the
Spiralized
Kitchen

the Spiralized Kitchen

Transform Your Vegetables into Fresh and Surprising Meals

Leslie Bilderback

Author of *Mug Cakes*

PHOTOGRAPHS BY TERI LYN FISHER

ST. MARTIN'S GRIFFIN
NEW YORK

To the fun and funny culinary specialists who welcomed me aboard the USS *Nitze* and the USS *Blue Ridge* in 2014. In between tasting international salts, learning about umami, and trying to improve the overall chow-line offerings, I was in my stateroom working on this book. Thanks for the great times!

THE SPIRALIZED KITCHEN. Copyright © 2015 by Leslie Bilderback. All rights reserved. Printed in the U.S.A. For information, address St. Martin's Press, 175 Fifth Avenue, New York, N.Y. 10010.

www.stmartins.com

Book design by Rita Sowins / Sowins Design
Photographs by Teri Lyn Fisher

The Library of Congress Cataloging-in-Publication Data is available upon request.

ISBN 978-1-250-06719-7 (trade paperback)
ISBN 978-1-4668-7520-3 (e-book)

St. Martin's Griffin books may be purchased for educational, business, or promotional use. For information on bulk purchases, please contact the Macmillan Corporate and Premium Sales Department at 1-800-221-7945, extension 5442, or write to specialmarkets@macmillan.com.

First Edition: March 2015

10 9 8 7 6 5 4 3 2 1

Contents

Main Events

Sides

Baking & Desserts

the basics

Welcome to the Spiralized Kitchen. These pages are intended to acquaint you not only with the possibilities of the spiralizer, but with your own creative possibilities. What follows are over 100 ideas for healthy, delicious, and fun ways to energize your menus.

What is a Spiralizer?

The spiralizer is a kitchen tool, similar to a grater, designed to make long, noodle-like ribbons out of vegetables and fruits. Spiralizers are fairly new, but fancifully shaped fruits and vegetables are very old. The classic kitchen station responsible for vegetable carving is called Garde Manger. In certain areas of the food service industry—fine dining, cruise ships, large hotels, culinary schools—and in the hand of its masters, vegetable carving is high art. As such, there were already tools available for the creative cook before the spiralizer hit the market. Until recently, long, noodle-shaped vegetables were created with a paring knife, a vegetable peeler, or a mandolin. If you don't have a spiralizer, these old-time, tried-and-true methods are perfectly adequate.

Who is the Spiralizer for?

Besides people who just like gadgets, and those who like fun-shaped food, the spiralizer has been marketed to those looking for ways to replace starchy, high carbohydrate pasta with something more healthful. Carbs have long been touted as a food to be avoided (thanks to Dr. Atkins), and this trend has been boosted by the recent onslaught of gluten-free foods. Whether you have a real aversion to gluten, or you're just looking for a way to add more vegetables to your diet, a spiralized meal is fun and healthy.

The recipes in this book will definitely help you add more vegetables and fruits to your menus. But you will not be able to successfully trick anyone into mistaking these recipes for pasta dishes—nor should you. They are clearly made with vegetables or fruits, and should be presented as such. Why? Because they should be eaten and enjoyed! Trying to trick someone into eating veggies and fruits will not cultivate an appreciation; it will only build resentment toward them—and you. So be honest with your eaters, and enjoy these spiralized recipes for what they are—beautiful and delicious.

Choosing Your Spiralizer

If you are setting out to purchase a spiralizer, you will find several options on the market. Regardless of the make and model, pay attention to a few key attributes when choosing one:

✳ SAFETY

Look for spiralizers that easily advance the vegetable through the mechanism, without forcing your fingers to come in contact with the blade. There should be a safety guard or handle that lets you push the produce through without touching the sharp cutting edge.

✳ UNIFORMITY AND SPEED

The spiralizer should easily create shapes of even thickness with little effort: You should not have to work hard to push the produce through, and the resulting shapes should be the same every time. If the blade bends out of shape after spiralizing your first carrot, the device is no good.

✳ EASY TO USE AND CLEAN

Too many parts make any gadget cumbersome. If you need to refer to the instruction manual every time you use your spiralizer, it's probably too complicated. And if you are anything like me, difficulty of operation or cleanup is a deal breaker.

✳ PRICE

As with most products, price is a good indication of quality—you get what you pay for. That said, there are some very durable spiralizers that come pretty cheap. I suggest you check the myriad reviews posted online for the best indication of quality.

B C

A D

Styles

1   The simplest and least expensive spiralizer is the handheld model. There are several makers, and as with most things, the price often determines reliability and durability. These look and work essentially like a big pencil sharpener, and can produce two "noodle" sizes. They are perfect for foods like zucchini, carrots, and cucumbers. But if your vegetable isn't thin and long, this model is useless. (For example, it is near impossible to spiralize a beet with this model.) (See photo A.)

2   The tabletop spiralizers offer three blade options, and can create not only long, thin or thick "noodles," but thin, flat corkscrews. This model is the more reliable tool, and the one I find most durable. It sticks to your counter with suction cups, and the vegetables advance through the blade easily on a sliding platform with the help of a handle that is oriented away from the blade. It is also surprisingly easy to clean and store, considering that it has several parts. (See photos B, C.)

3   Another model with several interchangeable blades is operated like a handheld food mill. It offers a few more shape sizes than the tabletop model, but is less durable, and a little harder to use because it is held in the hand rather than suctioned to the table.

4   There is also a handheld julienne peeler that works like a potato peeler. This tool is ideal for oddly shaped produce, and is great for really firm vegetables that might otherwise damage a more expensive tool. The downside to this model is that it does not create long spirals, but rather straight julienne strips that are only as long as the vegetable. (See photo D.)

5   The mandolin, also sometimes known as a "V" slicer, is a manual slicing machine. It became a crucial part of the professional kitchen in the early 1970s, and has features even the spiralizer doesn't, including a waffle-chip attachment, which is super fun. However, like the handheld julienne peeler, the strips created by the mandolin are only as long as the vegetable itself.

Spiralizing Technique

Once you have picked your spiralizer, there are a few tips to learn before you start spiralizing fruits and vegetables.

✳ FIRM AND SEEDLESS

Produce with firm, solid flesh make the best "noodles." For instance, the flesh of a zucchini is fairly solid throughout, and makes a better long noodle than yellow crook-neck squash, which has larger seeds in its soft center cavity. Anything soft and juicy, like tomatoes, are messy and the result you'll achieve is no better than what you might get if you simply used a knife.

✳ SIZE COUNTS

Small produce, like radishes, are dangerous to spiralize unless your spiralizer has a protective guard for your hand. The tabletop models work best for many smaller sized fruits and vegetables, but often you are left with more waste than useable spirals. Look for the larger versions of these small vegetables.

Large produce is also difficult. Usually it needs to be cut in halves or in chunks to fit into the spiralizer. Refer to the list on pages 8–13 for tips and techniques for spiralizing specific fruits and veggies.

✳ TO PEEL OR NOT TO PEEL

The nutrients in fruits and vegetables are close to the skin. If that isn't a good enough reason to keep the peel on, consider how much waste is created by peeling. (The best cooks always minimize waste!) Peeling the outer layer of a vegetable is recommended only when the skin is too tough to eat, or doesn't soften appreciably with cooking, as with a butternut squash or kohlrabi. Usually a good scrubbing is all that's necessary to remove dirt. Some organic produce, like yellow rainbow carrots, can be noticeably darker on the outside even when scrubbed clean. In this case I will peel off the discolored areas. But for the most part, I spiralize unpeeled. This includes fruits like apples and peaches, which I think look prettier with a tiny bit of skin still attached.

Cooking Tips

When cooking spiralized vegetables and fruits, remember that they cook quickly. Really quickly! Vegetables should be cooked until just tender, but not so tender that the noodle falls apart. The goal is to keep the length intact.

When sautéing long vegetable noodles, I recommend a traditional sauté pan. Its slanted sides allow you to stir what you're cooking with a flip of the wrist. The more you use a spoon to stir, the more your noodles will break. A wok is another good choice, because it has a wide surface area as well as slanted sides.

Boiling is often used to pre-soften harder produce, such as pumpkins and potatoes. It doesn't take long to soften such varieties, so watch them carefully. Roasting is also speedy, so keep a close eye on harder produce when you roast it as well. Thin edges can easily burn in the oven, so occasional stirring is recommended.

Produce Specifics

The following list offers tips and techniques for spiralizing specific fruits and veggies:

✳ APPLES

The best machine for spiralizing an apple is the tabletop model. For the best result, cut the apple in half across the fruit's equator, remove the seeds (a melon baller works well for this), and start spiralizing from the cut end, which will leave you with less waste and more large spirals. If you try to cut your apple in smaller spears for the handheld model, your spirals will turn out short rather than long and many will break.

Apples oxidize (turn brown) fairly quickly after they have been cut, so if your intention is to store your apple spirals for a period of time, submerge them in acidulated water. (This is water with some acid in it—usually lemon juice. A half lemon per gallon of water is sufficient.) However, if your apple spirals are going to be baked or caramelized they will turn brown anyway, so don't bother.

✳ BANANAS
Don't bother trying to spiralize a banana, unless it is very green. (Not that you would want to eat a very green banana.) Ripe bananas make a real mess in the spiralizer. Instead, use plantains, which are often preferable green. (See below.)

✳ BEETS
For beets, the tabletop model is the best. But do not cut the beet in half like the apple, unless you like cleaning up bright red beet juice. (It would be weird if you did.) And when you work with red beets, if you are spiralizing other produce, do the beets last so they don't stain everything else. It also pays to have a bowl or pan ready when the beets are cut—the longer they sit around once cut, the more they ooze their staining juice.

✳ BROCCOLI
There is no good way to spiralize broccoli florets, but you can spiralize the stems, which are quite lovely. The stems are skinny, so the handheld model should work.

✳ BUTTERNUT SQUASH
The seeds of the butternut squash are in the bottom bulbous portion, while the upper neck is solid. Therefore, it is the upper neck that produces the best spirals. To spiralize a butternut squash, cut off the neck, peel it with a knife or strong peeler, and use the tabletop spiralizer. If you have only the handheld version, cut the neck into long chunks, about the size of a zucchini. To use the bottom seeded portion of the squash, peel it, cut it in half across its equator, scoop out the seeds, then attach it to the tabletop spiralizer with the open end toward the blade. (Or cut into long chunks if you have the handheld model.) You will not get continuous long noodles, but there are some useable parts.

✳ CABBAGE
Spiralizing cabbage can be messy, and might hardly seem worth it. The trick is to pick the right head. Choose a small cabbage head, because the heavier it is, the harder it is for the plastic teeth of a spiralizer to hold it in place. And choose a tight head. If the leaves are loose, they will unravel from the core as you spin.

To spiralize, cut the small, tight head in half around its equator, and attach it to the tabletop spiralizer with its cut end facing the blade. If all you have is the handheld model, using a knife to shred the cabbage is much easier.

✳ CARROTS

You can use any model of spiralizer for a carrot, but the handheld model takes much more effort. Be careful, too, not to bend your handheld spiralizer out of shape when using this hard root. For best results, use a younger, more tender carrot.

✳ CELERY ROOT

Also known as celeriac, this root, along with the spice celery seed, comes from a different variety of celery than the one you smear with peanut butter. To spiralize celeriac, peel the root first, as the skin is tough. When using a tabletop model I suggest cutting the root in half across its equator, and facing the cut edge against the blade. For the handheld version, I cut it into zucchini-sized spears. Celeriac is commonly eaten raw in salads (most famously in Celery Root Remoulade, page 42), but can also be cooked like potatoes. Both are highly recommended.

✳ CUCUMBER

The best cucumbers for spiralizing, regardless of your tool, are English or Persian cucumbers. They work great in any machine because their seeds are few, their skin is thin, and their flesh is firm. Generic, fat, waxy-skinned cucumbers are too watery in the seed cavity, which causes them to fall apart when shredded. I am partial to the Persian variety, because they are small, firm, and cheap. The English cucumber works great, too, but is a bit pricier.

✳ EGGPLANT

As with all vegetables you might want to use with a spiralizer, firmer is better. But even firm eggplant can be challenging, because its flesh is soft and spongy. The only success I've had is with the single flat blade of the tabletop model, which makes great corkscrew ribbons, perfect for layering in veggie lasagna (Chapter 5), eggplant parmesan (Chapter 6), or simply roasted with olive oil and garlic. I found that long Chinese eggplant works better than the larger round eggplant, but both will work if the vegetable is young and fresh.

✳ FENNEL

The fennel bulb (sometimes sold as "sweet anise") is a great candidate for spiralizing with the single blade attachment of the tabletop model. To prepare, cut off the stems (save the lacy leaves for garnish!) and attach it to a spiralizer with the stem end facing the blade. Unfortunately, the vegetable is too fibrous and layered for any of the thinner "noodle" or julienne blades.

✳ JICAMA

Jicamas are firm and crunchy, which makes them perfect for spiralizing. To begin, peel the vegetable, then, for the tabletop models, cut it in half across its equator, and face the cut edge against the blade. For the handheld version, cut it into zucchini-sized spears. Jicama is usually eaten raw, and will become extra crisp if you store it in cold water in the fridge for at least 30 minutes.

✳ KOHLRABI

This misunderstood member of the vegetable kingdom is underused and underappreciated. Often mistaken for a root, kohlrabi is actually a swollen stem of a plant in the cabbage family. It tastes somewhat like a broccoli stem, with a firmer texture. Before spiralizing, peel away the tough outer skin, as it doesn't soften much when cooked. Because of its shape, the best spiralizer to use for kohlrabi is the tabletop model, unless you cut it into spears first.

✳ MELONS

Soft and juicy, melons are a terrible candidate for the spiralizer. But a firm melon can be processed into strips or ribbons using a handheld potato or julienne peeler. To prepare, peel the entire melon, then use your tool to strip away the sweet fruit from the outside in. Do this very close to serving time, though, because thinly cut melon becomes limp and translucent fairly quickly.

✳ ONIONS

Red, white, and yellow onions can be spiralized using a tabletop model. But because of their multiple layers, onions don't do well when spiralized as a sphere. To spiralize an onion, cut it in half at the equator and attach to the machine with the cut end toward the blade. This will also work with large shallots. Using a handheld spiralizer would require cutting the onion into spears, and is not recommended; it will literally bring you to tears.

✳ PARSNIPS

This vegetable, which looks like a white carrot, can be spiralized just like a carrot, in any type of spiralizer. Be aware, though, of old parsnips that are much less firm and less crisp than carrots. (Since parsnips are less popular, they tend to sit on the shelves longer and lose their freshness.) A limp parsnip will be a little more difficult to spiralize, but it can be done. Crisp them in a bowl of cold water in the fridge for at least 30 minutes, both before and after spiralizing.

✳ PEAR

The best way to spiralize a pear is by using the tabletop model. Choose fruit that is ripe, but still firm. Bosc pears are a great choice for this, because they stay very firm when ripe. To begin, remove the seeds at the center of the bulbous bottom of the fruit. I use a melon baller for this step, scooping out from the bottom up. Slice off the stem and attach the pear to the spiralizer with the stem end facing the blade. Pears do not oxidize as quickly as apples, but they do turn brown eventually, so prolonged storage of sliced pears should be in acidulated water.

✳ PEPPERS

Anything that is hollow is difficult to spiralize, but it is possible to spiralize bell peppers with the tabletop model. Just use the single blade for flat ribbons if they are large, fresh, and firm. Cut them in half at their equator, scoop out the seeds, and place the cut edge facing the blade.

✳ PLANTAIN

The plantain is a member of the banana family, but is less sweet. Plantains are usually used in savory applications as a starch, because the flavor is most reminiscent of potatoes. When ripe, the skin of the plantain is black. But a ripe plantain, though still more firm than a ripe banana, is very difficult to spiralize. The single blade of the tabletop model is your best bet for these softer fruits. If you need plantain strings choose a green, firm plantain. This is the standard choice for traditional *tostones*, the inspiration for the Fried Plantain recipe on page 19.

✳ POTATOES

The best way to spiralize a potato is on a tabletop machine, because the strings or curls will be long and uncut. That said, a large potato can be cut into spears and processed through the handheld device. Russet, new, white, red, and fingerling potatoes will oxidize after they are cut. If you don't plan to use the spirals right away, submerging them in water will prevent discoloration. Unlike apples, though, potatoes do not need acid in their water to prevent browning. Sweet potatoes, yams, and purple potatoes will not brown, but they will dry out fairly quickly, which is a good reason to store them in water once they are spiralized.

✳ PUMPKIN

See Winter Squash.

✳ SUMMER SQUASH

Summer squashes, thin skinned and tender, include zucchini, yellow, crook-neck, patty pan, and a number of other specimens with variegated coloration. All may be treated like zucchini (see below). However, beware of the more bulb-shaped versions (like the crook-neck). They will have a soft center seed cavity that does not spiralize as attractively as the zucchini.

✳ WINTER SQUASH

The easiest winter squash to spiralize is the butternut. Everything else is difficult to peel, and has a large hollow cavity filled with seeds. But, with a little effort, pumpkins, acorn squash, and kabocha squash can be spiralized. To prepare, peel the skin, cut the squash in half around its equator, and clean out the seed cavity. Then either cut it into spears for the handheld machine, or attach it to the tabletop spiralizer with the cut side toward the blade.

✳ ZUCCHINI

This is the most popular vegetable in the world of spiralizing. Firm but tender, with a soft edible skin and noticeably few seeds, it works with any model machine, and every blade. Like most vegetables, small and tender zucchini is preferable. That said, every gardener on Earth has produced a behemoth zucchini at one time or another. These giant specimens should be cut in half (at least) to fit into the tabletop machine, and in wedges for the handheld model. Before using, wash them well, but don't bother peeling—the skin is beautiful and delicious.

Now that you are fully versed in the idiosyncrasies of the spiralizer, prepare to be amazed!

appetizers & snacks

The word appetizer *has a formal connotation, and the recipes in this chapter will certainly fit that bill. But I have also added the title "snacks" because I am a firm believer that things don't need to be formal to be special—or delicious. Any of the recipes in this chapter would be welcome as an afterschool snack, a TV movie nosh, or a football halftime treat.*

Carrot and Parsnip Satay Skewers

MAKES ABOUT 2 DOZEN SMALL SKEWERS

Satay is originally an Indonesian dish of skewered meats in a savory peanut sauce. It has analogues throughout Asia, Africa, and the Middle East, but in the United States it is usually associated with Thai cuisine. Here, I have omitted the meat altogether, and used the sauce to impart a savory umami quality to two of the sweeter root vegetables. If you are a carnivore, see the variations below.

Ingredients

3 large carrots, peeled
3 large parsnips, peeled
¼ cup peanut butter
1 tablespoon soy sauce
1 tablespoon Sriracha sauce
Grated zest and juice of
   1 lime, plus extra lime
   wedges for garnish
1 tablespoon peanut or
   vegetable oil
1 clove garlic, minced
1 green onion, minced
¼ cup cilantro, chopped
¼ cup shelled peanuts,
   finely chopped

Method

1. Using the spiralizer with a straight blade, create flat spiral ribbons of the carrots and the parsnips. Submerge vegetable ribbons in two separate bowls of cold water, and set aside.

2. In a small bowl combine peanut butter, soy sauce, lime zest and juice, and Sriracha. Whisk together, adding enough water (2–4 tablespoons) to make a smooth sauce.

3. In a large sauté pan, heat the oil over medium heat. Add the carrots and sauté until just tender, about 1–2 minutes. Carefully remove from the pan, repeat with the parsnips. In remaining oil, add garlic and green onions, and sauté until just tender, but not brown. Remove from heat.

4. Add onion and garlic to the bowl of sauce. Stir to combine. Add carrots, parsnips, cilantro, and toss gently to coat well.

(continued)

5. To assemble skewers, fold carrots and parsnips in a fan pattern, skewering through the fat center portion of each strip as you fold. Alternate carrots and parsnips on each skewer.

6. To serve, place finished skewers on a platter, drizzle with remaining sauce, sprinkle with chopped peanuts, and garnish with lime wedges.

VARIATION

Chicken Satay: Toss chicken in remaining dressing, skewer as with the root vegetables, and cook on a grill or under the broiler. Serve with accompanying carrot and parsnip skewers. Try the same method with shrimp.

Fried Plantains

These are modeled after tostones, a dish that came to the New World with enslaved people from West Africa, and remained a popular dish in many Caribbean and Latin American countries. This recipe is similar in that it also uses green plantains, that are fried. But tostones are fried, smashed with a wooden tostonera plantain smasher (or a meat mallet, or the bottom of a cup), and fried again to fully cook and crisp the unripened fruit. Because the spiralizer creates such thin strips, if they were fried twice they would burn. This makes them slightly less fatty, but no less delicious.

Ingredients

¼ cup olive oil

½ large red onion, minced

1 small red chile pepper
   (such as a serrano),
   minced, or ½ teaspoon of
   cayenne pepper

2 cloves garlic, minced

1 teaspoon fresh oregano,
   chopped

1 teaspoon fresh thyme,
   picked from stem and
   chopped

½ teaspoon ground cumin

Grated zest and juice of
   1 lime

1 cup orange juice

¼ teaspoon freshly ground
   black pepper

Kosher salt, to taste

Method

1. For the dipping sauce, heat a large sauté pan over medium heat. Add oil, then onion and chile, and cook until tender and translucent, about 30 seconds. Add garlic, oregano, thyme, and cumin. Cook another 30 seconds, then remove from heat. Stir in lime zest and juice, and orange juice. Season with pepper and salt as needed, then set aside to macerate at room temperature.

2. In a small bowl, spiralize the plantains into thin shreds using the smallest holes. Toss with salt.

3. Preheat ¼ inch of oil in a large sauté pan over high heat. When hot, scoop up walnut-sized portions of the plantain spirals and set each gently into the oil. Do not crowd the pan. Flatten slightly and fry until golden and crispy, about 1–2 minutes on each side. Remove from the pan and transfer to a paper towel to drain while you repeat with the rest of the plantains. Serve hot with dipping sauce.

(continued)

Fried Plantains *(continued)*

4 firm plantains

1 tablespoon kosher salt

½–1 cup peanut or vegetable oil

VARIATIONS

Accompaniments: You can also serve these with guacamole, bean dip, sour cream, or your favorite salsa. They also make a lovely canapé topped with the chunky bits of the dipping sauce, or your best pico de gallo.

Yucca: Replace the plantain with peeled yucca, another starchy root with properties similar to a potato.

Cucumber-Caviar Canapés

MAKES ABOUT 3 DOZEN CANAPÉS

There is no doubt that the caviar makes this classic, elegant recipe so special. Caviar is definitely a delicacy, not to mention an acquired taste. Technically the salt-cured roe of Caspian or Black Sea sturgeon, "caviar" can refer to the roe of various fish species from many regions of the world. Sample a few, and use your favorite. You can substitute capers, or leave your cucumber roses plain, garnished with a tiny dill sprig.

Ingredients

¼ cup fresh dill, chopped

Grated zest and juice of 1 lemon

½ teaspoon kosher salt

2 tablespoons sour cream

3 large English or Persian cucumbers

10 sandwich slices brioche, pain de mie, or whole wheat bread

8 ounces cream cheese, softened

1 ounce of the best caviar you can afford

Method

1. In a large bowl combine dill, lemon zest and juice, salt, and sour cream. Stir to combine.

2. Spiralize unpeeled, unseeded cucumbers using the straight blade to create flat spiral ribbons. Put them in a container of cold water and refrigerate.

3. Toast each slice of bread until golden brown, in a toaster or on a dry baking sheet in the oven. Cool completely. At this point, the elements can be set aside (cucumber and dressing in the refrigerator, toast wrapped airtight at room temperature) for up to 24 hours, and assembled at the last minute.

4. To assemble canapés, slice the crust off the toast and cut into four triangle quarters. (These are called "toast points" by the pros.) Dollop or pipe a small amount of cream cheese in the center of each toast point.

5. Toss together drained cucumber and dressing. Roll cucumber ribbons into decorative rose shapes, and place one on each toast point. Place a tiny portion of caviar on top of each cucumber rose. Arrange canapés on a clean platter, leaving about ½ inch between each.

Cucumber-Jicama Shrimp Ceviche

MAKES ABOUT 4 SERVINGS

Despite common belief, ceviche is not raw fish. It is a dish made from fish that has been cooked with acid. Acid denatures (or tightens) the protein in the same way that heat does. This dish is popular in cultures with access to abundant seafood. There are as many regional variations as there are coastlines. This version is my favorite, but I have added a few others in the variations section below.

Ingredients

1 pound medium shrimp, shelled, deveined, and chopped in ½-inch chunks

Grated zest and juice of 3 limes

1 large English or Persian cucumber

1 small jicama

1–3 jalapeño peppers, to taste

½ red bell pepper, diced

½ yellow bell pepper, diced

1 large tomato, diced

1 cup fresh cilantro leaves

Grated zest and juice of 1 orange

2 tablespoons olive oil

Method

1. Combine the cleaned and chopped shrimp with the lime zest and juice, and set aside in the refrigerator to cook for 30–60 minutes.

2. Spiralize cucumber and jicama into thin shreds using the smallest holes. Combine in a large bowl of cold water and refrigerate.

3. Seed and mince jalapeño (as many as you can handle), and place in a separate bowl. Add the diced red and yellow bell peppers, tomato, and cilantro. Add orange zest and juice, oil, cumin, coriander, salt, and pepper. Toss until well coated.

4. Once shrimp is pink and firm (in other words, cooked), strain off lime juice and add to the bowl of peppers. Add cucumber and jicama. Toss, taste, and adjust seasoning as needed. Toss in avocado just before serving in cocktail or parfait glasses.

1 teaspoon ground cumin

½ teaspoon ground coriander

1 teaspoon kosher salt

½ teaspoon freshly ground black pepper

1 large ripe avocado, diced

VARIATIONS

Seafood Options: Ceviche is nice with mild whitefish such as tilapia, cod, or sole. Or try it with fresh calamari. Salmon and tuna are great if you like the stronger flavors. Whichever fish you choose, be sure it's fresh.

Avocado Bowl: Remove the pit from a large ripe avocado. Scoop out a little bit of the fruit to use in the recipe, then pile the finished ceviche high in the avocado. Try the same method using a large tomato.

Citrus Explosion: After the shrimp is cooked and the lime juice has been drained off, add the grated zest of a lemon, and the chopped sections of a blood orange, pink grapefruit, or pomelo.

Curried Potato Bites

MAKES 2 TO 3 DOZEN POTATO BITES

Curry and potatoes are a classic combination. This recipe makes a great snack as is, or top them with the chutney recipe that follows. Delish! There are many variations of curry spice blend. Feel free to use your favorite.

Ingredients

1 russet potato
1 sweet potato
1 tablespoon olive oil
3 green onions, chopped
2 tablespoons garam
    masala curry spice or
    paste blend
1 teaspoon kosher salt
½ teaspoon freshly ground
    black pepper

Method

1. Preheat oven to 350° F. Spiralize the potatoes into thin shreds using the smallest holes. In a large bowl, combine them with olive oil, green onions, garam masala, salt and pepper.

2. Coat a muffin tin with pan spray. Gather up spiralized potato mixture into ¼-cup bundles and arrange them in each muffin tin. Bake until golden and crisp, about 10–20 minutes. Remove from the oven and cool for 5 minutes before removing from the tins.

3. Serve immediately, topped with a teaspoon of chutney (see recipe on page 28), sour cream, or plain yogurt.

VARIATION

Veggie Variation: You can make these potato bites using any number of root vegetables. Create a colorful mix by choosing sweet and white potatoes, or carrots and parsnips.

Quick Mango Chutney

MAKES ABOUT 1 QUART

You can make this chutney two or three days ahead. In fact, it tastes best if it has some time to macerate. It also freezes well for up to a month, so make a double batch and use it for your next Indian feast.

Ingredients

1 cup golden raisins

1 tablespoon vegetable oil

1 small red onion

1 teaspoon chile flakes

1 ripe mango, diced (or 2 cups frozen mango chunks, defrosted)

1 tablespoon freshly grated ginger root

1 cup pineapple juice

¼ cup cider vinegar

¼ cup honey

½ cup fresh cilantro leaves, chopped

1 teaspoon ground cumin

½ teaspoon kosher salt

Method

1. Cover the raisins with boiling water and set aside at room temperature to plump for at least 15 minutes. (You can also plump the raisins by soaking overnight in cold water.)

2. In a large sauté pan heat the oil over medium heat. Add onions, chile flakes, and cook until translucent. Add mango, ginger, and cook, stirring, until soft, about 2 minutes.

3. Slowly add the pineapple juice, vinegar, and honey, and continue cooking at a simmer, stirring occasionally, for about 15 minutes, until the mixture resembles a chunky jam.

4. Remove from the heat. Stir in raisins, cilantro, cumin, and salt. Set aside to cool completely. Store refrigerated, or freeze for up to a month.

Parsnip Chips with Green Goddess Dip

MAKES ABOUT 4 SERVINGS

Green Goddess dressing is not, as some believe, made from avocados. It is an herb-based dressing that originated in San Francisco's Palace Hotel in the 1920s, created to honor a popular theater production of the time, entitled The Green Goddess. *(#TheMoreYouKnow)*

Ingredients

1 anchovy filet
1 clove garlic
1 cup mayonnaise
½ cup fresh Italian parsley leaves
¼ cup fresh tarragon or mint leaves
¼ cup fresh basil leaves
2 green onions
Grated zest and juice of 1 lemon
½ teaspoon kosher salt
½ teaspoon fresh ground black pepper
4 large parsnips
2 tablespoons olive oil
½ teaspoon kosher salt

Method

1. To make the dressing, combine in a blender the anchovy, garlic, mayo, herbs, green onions, lemon juice and zest, salt and pepper. Blend until smooth, adjust seasoning, and store in the refrigerator.

2. Preheat oven to 375° F. Using the spiralizer with a straight blade, create flat spiral ribbons of parsnip. Toss in a large bowl with oil, then spread onto a baking sheet in an even layer. Bake for 10–15 minutes. Stir the parsnips around the sheet pan after 5 minutes to promote even cooking. When they're done the parsnips should be golden brown and crisp on the edges. Sprinkle with salt directly out of the oven. Let cool to room temperature to crisp, then serve with a side of Green Goddess for dipping.

VARIATION

Strings: You can make your parsnips into "curly fry" strings if you are using the handheld tool. Use the larger sized holes. Be careful not to overcook this thinner version. Cooking time will be shorter, and more stirring is necessary for even cooking.

Potato Nests

MAKES 6 TO 8 BASKETS

These make a great appetizer base to be filled with any number of things, although here I have kept it simple with an easy tomato salad. Try it with a breakfast egg-and-bacon scramble, creamed spinach as a side dish, or even your best homemade chili. You will need a bird's nest frying tool, which are available online for under ten dollars. If you don't have this, and are not interested in deep-frying, see the baked variation below.

Ingredients

1 pint cherry tomatoes, halved

¼ cup fresh basil, chopped

1 tablespoon olive oil

1 teaspoon balsamic vinegar

¼ teaspoon kosher salt

2–4 cups vegetable oil, depending on size of pan used

1 russet potato

1–2 teaspoons kosher salt

½ teaspoon freshly ground black pepper

¼ cup sour cream

Method

1. In a small bowl combine tomatoes, basil, olive oil, balsamic vinegar, and salt. Toss together and set aside to macerate at room temperature.

2. Heat oil in a large saucepan to 350° F. (Oil should be deep enough so that the basket is submerged.) Have at the ready a paper towel–lined tray.

3. In a large bowl, spiralize the potato into thin shreds using the smallest holes.

4. Gather up about ¼ cup of potatoes and arrange them in the bottom of the bird's nest fryer basket. Press the smaller basket into the potatoes and place it in the preheated oil. Fry until they begin to turn golden brown, about 1 minute. Remove the smaller top basket from oil and continue to cook the potatoes in oil to brown the interior.

5. When the center becomes golden, turn the basket upside down over the oil and tap the bottom of the basket to dislodge the potato basket back into the oil. (Hold the basket close to the oil to avoid splatter.) Cook until all traces of white potato disappear. Be careful not to overcook. Too dark and the potatoes will become bitter. If necessary, adjust the heat to keep the oil at 350° F. Remove

the basket to a paper towel to drain, and immediately sprinkle with salt. (It will help the salt stick, and absorbs remaining moisture, keeping the baskets crisp longer.) Repeat with remaining potatoes.

6. To prepare, arrange nests on a platter. Fill each with a tablespoon of tomato salad, and top with a dollop of sour cream and pepper, to taste. Serve immediately.

VARIATIONS

Veggie Variation: You can fry nests using any number of root vegetables, including carrot, parsnip, sweet potato, butternut squash, celery root, yucca, purple potato, and even plantain. But one word of warning: Mixing veggie strings in one basket is a bad idea. The different sugar levels of each root means that some will burn while others remain undercooked.

Oven Baked: If you'd like to avoid deep-frying, follow the procedure for the Curried Potato Bites on page 26. Though that recipe adds spice to the raw potatoes, you can leave them unseasoned, as above.

Rice Paper Spring Rolls

MAKES ABOUT 20 SPRING ROLLS

These spring rolls are fresh, healthy, and deceptively filling. Just because they are in the appetizer section doesn't mean you can't have them for lunch, too! Rice paper sheets are available in Asian markets, or online.

Ingredients

1 tablespoon sesame oil

2 tablespoons soy sauce

1 tablespoon honey

2 tablespoons rice vinegar

1-2 tablespoons Sriracha sauce (optional, but delicious!)

1 zucchini

1 medium English or Persian cucumber

1 medium daikon radish

1¼ head cabbage (Savoy or regular green), shredded fine with a knife

1 red bell pepper, diced fine

2 green onions, chopped fine

2 tablespoons freshly grated ginger root

1 cup fresh cilantro leaves

10—15 long chives or chive blossoms (optional)

1 package (about 20 pieces) rice paper sheets

Method

1. In a large bowl combine sesame oil, soy sauce, honey, vinegar, and Sriracha. Set aside at room temperature.

2. Spiralize zucchini, cucumber, and daikon into thin shreds using the smallest holes. Combine them in a large bowl with the cabbage, red pepper, green onions, ginger, and cilantro. Add the dressing, toss to combine, and season to taste. Set aside.

3. Fill a large bowl or baking pan with 2–3 inches of cold water. Submerge one sheet of rice paper in the cold water until it transforms from rigid to soft and flexible, about 30 seconds. Remove from water and spread out flat on the counter, or a large plate. Gather up about ¼ cup of vegetable mixture and place it at the end of the rice paper, closest to you. If using chives or chive blossoms lay one across the top of the pile of veggies. Fold the bottom edge up and over the vegetables. Fold the right and left edges on top, then roll from the bottom up to encase the vegetables in a thin burrito-like form. Set aside and repeat with remaining vegetables and rice paper. Serve whole or sliced in half, and arrange on a platter. Store refrigerated for up to an hour before serving.

Roasted Fennel Crostini

MAKES ABOUT 10 TO 12 SERVINGS

Crostino means "little toast" in Italian, and this dish, which consists of toast with a variety of simple toppings, is probably a holdover from medieval diners who ate off of stale bread rather than plates. Though a modern crostini usually includes a tomato topping, this version takes advantage of the sweet, anise essence of fennel. See the variations below for more ideas.

Ingredients

1 long loaf French or Italian bread (baguette shaped), cut into ½-inch slices on the bias

½–1 cup olive oil, extra virgin or regular

3 bulbs fennel

1 yellow onion

2 garlic cloves, minced

Grated zest and juice of 1 large orange

1 tablespoon fennel seeds, toasted

1 teaspoon kosher salt

1 cup fennel fronds, minced

1 cup feta cheese, crumbled

Method

1. Preheat oven to 350° F. Arrange bread slices on a baking sheet, brush lightly with olive oil, and bake until lightly toasted, about 10 minutes. Remove from oven and set aside. Keep the oven on.

2. Spiralize fennel and onion into thin shreds using the smallest holes, and combine in a large bowl. Add garlic, orange zest and juice, and fennel seeds. Toss together with 2 tablespoons of olive oil, and salt. Spread out onto another baking sheet, and roast until golden and caramelized, about 10 minutes. Remove and cool enough to handle. Keep oven on.

3. Add the fennel fronds to the roasted fennel mixture and toss again to evenly distribute flavors. Top each slice of toast with about ¼ cup of the roasted fennel mixture, and a light sprinkle of feta cheese. Just before serving, return to the oven for 5 minutes to warm through. Arrange warmed bruschetta on a platter and serve.

Cheese Options: Swap the feta cheese with goat cheese for a more pungent version. Or try a thin slice of brie, manchego, or fontina.

Tomato: Traditional bruschetta is tomato based, and this recipe is only enhanced by them. Find the ripest, freshest (preferably homegrown) tomatoes you can. Seed and dice them, and toss them into the fennel mixture. Or try it with halved red or yellow cherry tomatoes.

Apple-Caraway: Apples and fennel are a great pair. Add a spiralized apple to this mixture. Substitute the fennel with toasted caraway seeds if you'd like a more savory version.

Spiralized Vegetable Sushi

MAKES 8 TO 10 ROLLS

Sushi is most definitely an art form, but that doesn't mean you can't do it. (I'm not an artist, but I still like to sketch.) The basic concept is actually pretty easy, and once you've mastered the technique, the possibilities are endless. A real sushi rolling mat is useful, but not essential. In a pinch I have used a small towel or washcloth, wrapped in plastic.

Ingredients

2 cups sushi rice

1 tablespoon sugar

1 teaspoon rice vinegar

1 zucchini

1 yellow squash

1 carrot

1 medium English or
    Persian cucumber

1 red bell pepper

1 avocado

8–10 sheets nori seaweed

1 cup soy sauce

1–2 tablespoons wasabi

½ cup pickled ginger slices

Method

1. In a large saucepan bring 4 cups of water to a boil over high heat. Rinse sushi rice in cold water 2–3 times until the water runs clear, then add it to the boiling water. The water will go still, then come back up to the boil. Reduce the heat to a simmer, cover, and cook for 20 minutes on low heat, just until the water is absorbed.

2. Transfer warm cooked rice to a large bowl. In a small bowl, combine sugar and vinegar, and stir until sugar dissolves, then toss it into the rice. Fold the sugar-vinegar mixture into the rice until well coated. Sushi chefs do this while fanning to help it cool. Spread rice out onto a baking sheet and let it cool at room temperature.

3. Spiralize zucchini, yellow squash, carrot, cucumber, and red bell pepper into thin shreds using the smallest holes. Keep each spiralized vegetable separated. Slice avocado into thin strips.

4. Place one sheet of nori onto the sushi rolling mat. Press ¾–1 cup of sushi rice onto the nori in a thin, even layer, leaving ½ inch of nori uncovered at the top. Arrange an assortment of spiralized vegetables along the bottom edge of the rice, 2–3 strips of each vegetable should be enough. Add a thin strip of avocado.

5. Brush a little water along the top inch of uncovered nori. Roll the sushi mat, nori, and all the ingredients from the bottom up, stopping periodically to squeeze and tighten the roll. Set finished roll in the refrigerator while you repeat with remaining rice and vegetables.

6. When all rolls are complete, slice each into 1-inch coins. Serve immediately on a platter with an accompanying ramekin of soy sauce, a dollop of wasabi, and a small pile of pickled ginger.

VARIATIONS

Fish: Sushi rolls are great with the freshest raw tuna or salmon. Just be sure they are very fresh, super clean, and well chilled. Cooked shrimp, crab, octopus, and eel are also common fillings. Experiment!

Spicy Mayo: Mayonnaise is surprisingly popular in Japan. (It's a common pizza topping!) The easiest spicy mayo recipe is made by mixing together ½ cup mayo, 2 tablespoons of Sriracha, and a teaspoon of lime juice. Spread this on the rice before adding the veggies.

Sweet Potato-Stuffed Jalapeño Poppers

MAKES 20 SERVINGS

This is the ultimate bar food, and is best enjoyed with an ice-cold beer. Consider these for your next Super Bowl party! Gloves are recommended for this recipe, as hot peppers will spread their capsicum to your skin, and then to everything you touch.

Ingredients

20 jalapeño peppers

¼ cup olive oil

2 large sweet potatoes

1 clove garlic, minced

2 green onions, minced

4 ounces crumbled goat cheese

½ teaspoon kosher salt

¼ teaspoon freshly ground black pepper

Method

1. To prepare the jalapeños cut off the stem top, and use a sharp paring knife or a tiny melon baller to remove the seeds and inner membrane. Coat peppers inside and out with olive oil, and set aside.

2. Spiralize the sweet potatoes into thin shreds using the smallest holes. Slice potato strings into 1- or 2-inch lengths, and mix with remaining olive oil, garlic, onions, goat cheese, salt and pepper. The mixture should resemble a chunky paste.

3. Preheat oven to 375° F. Stuff the sweet potato mixture into each hollowed out jalapeño until it is full. Arrange in a single layer on a baking sheet. Bake until the peppers are charred and the potatoes are tender, about 30 minutes. Serve hot with an ice-cold beer.

> **VARIATION**
>
> **Cheese Choices:** If you are not a fan of goat cheese, use grated jack, cheddar, or cream cheese.

Salads

Fresh, crunchy, delicious, and good for you, it comes as no surprise that salads are the perfect canvas for spiralizing. There is no law that says a salad has to consist of lettuce and bottled dressing. Roots, fruits, and roasted veggies add a layer of interest to standard salad fare.

Celery Root Remoulade

MAKES ABOUT 4 LARGE SERVINGS

Remoulade sauce originated in France, which may explain its popularity in Louisiana. Though in many parts of the world it is used as a condiment for meat (in Iceland they put it on hot dogs), the French version is a simple herbed mayonnaise, perfect to enhance this unique root.

Ingredients

2 large celery roots (also called celeriac)

1 cup mayonnaise

1 tablespoon Dijon mustard

½ teaspoon prepared horse-radish

Grated zest and juice of 1 lemon

1 teaspoon kosher salt

½ teaspoon white pepper or freshly ground black pepper

¼ cup fresh Italian parsley leaves, chopped

1 tablespoon fresh chives, chopped

1 tablespoon fresh chervil, chopped

1 tablespoon fresh tarragon, chopped

Method

1. Spiralize the celery root into thin shreds using the smallest holes, then cut into 2- to 4-inch lengths. (These can be cut up to 24 hours ahead, and stored in cold water in the fridge.)

2. In a large bowl combine the mayonnaise, mustard, and horseradish. Stir in lemon zest and juice, salt, pepper and herbs. Add the celery root (remember to drain the water it's been soaking in) and toss well to evenly coat. Serve chilled.

VARIATIONS

Sweeten It Up: Replace one of the celery roots with 3 large apples (I prefer Fuji, but use your favorite.) Garnish with some chopped walnuts.

Salty Version: Many remoulade recipes contain chopped cornichons or capers. Add one tablespoon of each for a saltier, mouthwatering variation.

Creole: In Louisiana remoulade is red, and almost always used as an accompaniment to shrimp. Add some cooked chopped shrimp to this recipe, and spike your remoulade sauce with cayenne and paprika (or Cajun seasoning). It's not authentic, but it is delicious.

Cilantro-Lime Jicama Salad

MAKES ABOUT 4 LARGE SERVINGS

Jicama is a crisp and crunchy white root of a plant in the bean family (it is sometimes called the "yam bean"). The root has a papery light brown skin and a crunchy white interior that is similar to an apple in texture. Used extensively in Mexico, the jicama was spread by the Spanish to China, South East Asia, and the Philippines, where it has become a common ingredient in many of these cuisines.

Ingredients

2 tablespoons vegetable oil

Grated zest and juice of 2 limes

¼ cup agave syrup

1 red jalapeño chile, minced

½ teaspoon kosher salt

½ teaspoon fresh ground black pepper

1 large jicama

4–5 radishes

2 cups butter lettuce or green leaf lettuce, shredded

1 cup cilantro leaves whole

Method

1. In a large bowl combine the oil, lime zest and juice, agave, jalapeño, salt, pepper, and stir to combine.

2. Spiralize the jicama into thin shreds using the smallest holes, then add them to the dressing. Add the radishes and jalapeño, and toss to coat with dressing. Add lettuce, cilantro, and toss again. Serve chilled.

> **VARIATION**
>
> **Fruity:** Try this salad with an addition of crisp melon, mango, or papaya. Cut them into thin strips and add them at the end.

Beet and Balsamic Berry Salad

MAKES ABOUT 4 LARGE SERVINGS

Sweet, juicy beets are delicious and nutritious. They are super-sweet, and are one of the main sources of granulated sugar. But they pack a punch of folic acid, and their dark color hints at their antioxidant content. One word of caution: Their juice stains both hands and clothes, so consider wearing an apron!

Ingredients

3 large beets, including greens if possible

1 large red onion

4 tablespoons olive oil

Grated zest and juice of 1 orange

1 tablespoon fresh thyme, picked from stem and chopped

2 tablespoons balsamic vinegar

½ teaspoon kosher salt

½ teaspoon freshly ground black pepper

1 pint blackberries

1 pint raspberries

¼ cup pistachios, shelled and chopped

Method

1. Preheat oven to 350° F. Spiralize the beets into thin shreds using the smallest holes. Place them in a large bowl and toss with 1–2 tablespoons of olive oil to coat. Spread out in an even layer on a baking sheet and roast about 15 minutes, until tender but not dry. Cool completely.

2. Meanwhile, spiralize the red onion also into thin shreds using the smallest holes. Place them in a bowl of cold water and let soak for at least 15 minutes (or as long as overnight). This leaches out much of the bitter "bad breath" onion oils.

3. In a large bowl, combine 2 tablespoons of olive oil, orange zest and juice, thyme, vinegar, salt, and pepper. Stir to combine, then add berries, drained onions, and roasted beets. If you have reserved beet greens, chop them into a fine chiffonade and add. Toss well to evenly distribute ingredients, and divide between 4 plates. Top with pistachios, and serve.

(continued)

Beet and Balsamic Berry Salad *(continued)*

Note: How to Chiffonade

Chiffonade is a culinary term that refers to a julienne (or thin strip) of a leaf. To make a proper chiffonade, stack 3–4 leaves on top of each other, roll them up into a lengthwise cylinder, and then slice into tiny coins. The coins will unravel into herby ribbons. Voila!

VARIATIONS

Nutty Options: There are any number of nuts that can be used to compliment the sweet beets. If I don't have pistachios I opt for walnuts, pecans, or pine nuts—but by all means use your imagination!

Say Cheese: A tangy, pungent cheese would make a great addition to these sweet ingredients. Try crumbled goat, feta, or blue cheese.

Creamy Cabbage Slaw

MAKES ABOUT 6 SERVINGS

Good slaw is a fine art. There are plenty of so-so slaws, and everybody has their favorite. Mine is creamy, and just a little bit sweet.

Ingredients

¼ cup golden raisins

¼ cup dark raisins

½ cup sour cream

½ cup mayonnaise

1 tablespoon celery seed

1 teaspoon kosher salt

1 teaspoon fresh ground
   black pepper

1 8-ounce can crushed
   pineapple, with juice

1 small, tight head of green
   cabbage

1 large carrot

1 white onion

Method

1. In a small bowl combine golden and dark raisins, cover with boiling water, and set aside for at least 15 minutes—though longer is better—to plump. (You can also plump the raisins by soaking overnight in cold water.)

2. In a large bowl add the mayonnaise, celery seed, salt, pepper, and whisk together well. Fold in crushed pineapple and its juice.

3. Spiralize the onion and cabbage using the straight blade to create flat spiral ribbons. Add to the dressing and toss to coat. Spiralize the carrot into thin shreds using the smallest holes. Add them to the dressing as well, and toss again. Finally, drain the raisins, add them, and toss it all together. For maximum flavor, allow to macerate for 30–60 minutes at room temperature before serving.

VARIATIONS

Creamier Slaw: If you like an even creamier slaw, drain off the juice from the crushed pineapple and add ½ cup of sour cream to the dressing.

Spicy Slaw: If you like a bit of heat, add a tablespoon of prepared horseradish or wasabi. For this versions omit the raisins, and add some chopped peanuts or cashews.

Dilly Radish and Cucumbers

MAKES ABOUT 4 SERVINGS

This salad is perfect as is, but I have also been known to use it as a filling for tea sandwiches. If you have a farmers market nearby (or a green thumb), seek out some of the specialty radish varieties with pretty colors or stripes, like the "easter egg" or "watermelon" varieties. They make this already special salad extra special.

Ingredients

1 cup sour cream
1 tablespoon dried dill weed
¼ cup fresh dill, minced
¼ cup fresh chives, or 2 green onions, minced
Grated zest and juice of 1 lemon
½ teaspoon kosher salt
½ teaspoon fresh ground black pepper
6–8 large red or specialty radishes
2 medium English or Persian cucumbers

Method

1. In a large bowl whisk together the sour cream, dill weed, fresh dill, chives, lemon zest and juice, salt and pepper. Set aside.

2. Spiralize the radishes and cucumbers using the straight blade to create flat spiral ribbons. Add them to the dressing and toss well to coat evenly. Serve chilled or at room temperature.

> **VARIATIONS**
>
> **Watercress:** Try this classic tea sandwich combination. Toss 1–2 cups of watercress leaves and thin stems in with the cucumbers and radishes.
>
> **Daikon:** This fat white radish is just as crunchy and pungent as the little red variety, and works wonderfully here.
>
> **The Far East:** Radish and cucumber are used around the world. Give this recipe a Middle Eastern flair by replacing the dill with curly parsley, and adding a pinch of ground cumin. Or turn it into an Asian dish by using the dressing from the Spring Rolls recipe on page 32.

Spiralized Waldorf Salad

MAKES ABOUT 4 LARGE SERVINGS

This old-time original has a long history, and an even longer list of variations. It was created in the 1890s by the maître d'hôtel (not the chef!) of the Waldorf Astoria Hotel in New York City. Grapes and nuts are a later addition to this salad, first appearing in written form in the 1920s. They have since become de rigueur. *If you don't feel like buying two different colored grapes, it's fine to choose just one. Similarly, go ahead and use a fancy variety of seeded grapes. Just try to remove the seeds as best you can after they are halved.*

Ingredients

½ cup mayonnaise

Grated zest and juice of
   1 lemon

¼ teaspoon kosher salt

½ teaspoon fresh ground
   black pepper

2 cups walnut pieces,
   toasted

2 stalks celery, diced

1 cup red grapes, halved

1 cup green grapes, halved

3 Fuji apples (or your
   favorite snacking apple)

Method

1. In a large bowl combine the mayonnaise, lemon zest and juice, salt, and pepper. Add walnuts, celery, and grapes. Toss together to evenly coat.

2. Spiralize the apples into thin shreds using the smallest holes. Add the apples to the mayonnaise mixture, and toss again to coat. Chill for 15–30 minutes before serving.

VARIATION

Herbs: Add ½ cup of chopped fresh Italian parsley, chervil, or thyme. The herby addition bumps up this salad's sophistication.

Fennel Apple Salad with Rosemary and Raisins

MAKES ABOUT 4 SERVINGS

Fennel is one of my favorite flavors. Its licorice quality is subtle and sophisticated, and goes well with everything from sweet fruits to gamey meats. This salad improves with age. The apples oxidize a little, but don't let that deter you. It is 100 times better the morning after.

Ingredients

1 cup golden raisins

2 tablespoons olive oil

1 small yellow onion, diced

2 tablespoons fresh rosemary needles, pulverized in a coffee mill, or minced very fine

1 tablespoon cider or white wine vinegar

½ teaspoon kosher salt

½ teaspoon freshly ground black pepper

2 bulbs fennel (also known as sweet anise)

2 large Fuji apples (or your favorite not-too-tart apple)

Method

1. In a small bowl, cover golden raisins with boiling water and set aside for at least 15 minutes—longer is better—to plump. (You can also plump the raisins by soaking overnight in cold water.)

2. Warm oil in a small sauté pan over medium heat. Add onions and rosemary, and cook, stirring until onions just begin to color. Remove from heat and cool to room temperature. Stir in vinegar, salt and pepper, and set aside.

3. Spiralize fennel and apples into thin shreds using the smallest holes. Combine them in a large bowl with the cooled dressing, and toss to coat completely. Add raisins and allow to macerate for at least 15–30 minutes before serving chilled or at room temperature.

> **VARIATION**
>
> **Fennel Fronds:** If your fennel bulbs came with stems and the frilly fronds that look like dill, use them! Chop those delicate leaves and add them at the end, with the raisins.

Rainbow Carrot Salad

MAKES ABOUT 4 LARGE SERVINGS

Carrot salad is an American classic, but the use of rainbow carrots and a variety of dried fruits makes it new. Incidentally, carrots didn't start out orange. They were white and purple, until the royal botanist of the Dutch House of Orange got ahold of them.

Ingredients

½ cup golden raisins

½ cup dark raisins (consider using muscat raisins if you can find them)

¼ cup dried currants

½ cup mayonnaise

Grated zest and juice of 1 orange

½ teaspoon kosher salt

½ teaspoon freshly ground black pepper

2 green onions, chopped fine

6 large carrots, in a variety of colors

1–2 teaspoons lemon juice

Method

1. In a small bowl, combine golden raisins, dark raisins, and currants, cover with boiling water, and set aside for at least 15 minutes—longer is better—to plump. (You can also plump the raisins by soaking overnight in cold water.)

2. In a large bowl stir together mayonnaise, orange zest and juice, salt and pepper. Stir in green onions and set aside.

3. Spiralize carrots into thin shreds using the smallest holes. (This works nicely with the handheld julienne peeler, too.) Add them to the bowl of dressing, along with the drained raisin mixture. Toss well to combine, and season as needed with lemon juice or salt. Allow to macerate for at least 15 minutes at room temperature before serving.

VARIATIONS

Moroccan Carrots: To the mayonnaise, add 2 tablespoons of harissa, 1 clove chopped garlic, and a pinch each of cumin and cinnamon.

Apples: Add two apples to this recipe, spiralized in the same shape as the carrots.

Nutty: Nuts add a rich toastiness to this dish. Add toasted pecan or walnut pieces just before serving. Or try it with sunflower seeds!

Roasted Potato-Pecan Salad

MAKES ABOUT 4 LARGE SERVINGS

Potato salad is usually pretty humdrum. But this version takes advantage of the spiralized shape to roast the spuds, which lends a toasted, caramelized flavor.

Ingredients

2 cups pecan pieces

2 large russet potatoes

1 large yellow onion

2 tablespoons olive oil

1 clove garlic

1 teaspoon kosher salt

½ cup mayonnaise

Zest and juice of 1 lemon

1 teaspoon dried Herbes de
   Provence or dried thyme

Method

1. Preheat oven to 375°F. Spread pecans onto a baking sheet in a single layer and roast until toasty and fragrant, about 10 minutes. Pour off of baking sheet and set aside to cool.

2. Spiralize potatoes and onions using the straight blade to create flat spiral ribbons. Toss them with the olive oil in a large bowl, then spread them out on a baking sheet in an even layer. Roast until they are golden brown and tender, about 15 minutes. Cool to room temperature.

3. Mince the garlic on a cutting board along with the kosher salt. The salt crystals help draw out the moisture to make it more like a paste, and help leach out some of the bitterness. Place the minced garlic and salt in a large bowl. Add the mayonnaise, lemon zest and juice, and dried herbs. Stir to combine. Add the pecans, then the roasted potatoes and onions. Toss to coat evenly. Serve chilled or at room temperature.

Spiralized Greek Salad

MAKES ABOUT 4 LARGE SERVINGS

Greek salad is super refreshing on a hot summer day. But why wait until summer to enjoy it? The essential ingredients are available most of the year. So go ahead! Add a taste of summer on your next rainy day. Opa!

Ingredients

¼ cup olive oil, extra virgin
    or regular
2 tablespoons red wine
    vinegar
Grated zest and juice of
    1 lemon
½ teaspoon kosher salt
½ teaspoon fresh ground
    black pepper
¼ cup fresh oregano leaves,
    roughly chopped (or 1
    tablespoon dried oregano,
    crushed)
2 large English or Persian
    cucumbers
1 large green bell pepper
1 large red onion
1 cup Italian parsley
    leaves, whole
8 ounces feta cheese, cubed
1 large ripe tomato, diced,
    or 1 cup cherry tomatoes,
    halved
½ cup kalamata olives,
    pitted and roughly
    chopped

Method

1. In a large bowl whisk together oil, vinegar, lemon zest and juice, salt, pepper, and oregano. Set aside.

2. Spiralize the cucumbers and bell peppers using the straight blade to create flat spiral ribbons. Spiralize the red onion into thin shreds using the smallest holes. Add them to the bowl of dressing and toss to coat.

3. Add the parsley, feta, tomato, and olives to the bowl, and toss again. Allow the salad to macerate at room temperature for 15 minutes before serving for maximum flavor. Serve with crisp pita chips for a well-rounded lunch.

VARIATIONS

Herbs: Some versions of this salad use either dill or mint. Feel free to substitute these herbs, or use them all!

Green Olives: Though kalamata olives are the standard here, there are many delicious varieties of cured olives. It is the saltiness of them that is harnessed in this recipe, so go ahead and experiment!

Creamy Greek: If you like your dressing on the thick side, add to this recipe ½ cup of plain Greek yogurt.

Soups

*Because the spiralizer creates long
vegetable noodles, it seems only natural
to use it for soup, which is a frequent
bearer of noodles. But once you start
spiralizing, it's hard to stop, which is
why some of the soups I've included
don't usually have noodles at all.
Spiralizing is irresistible.*

Beef Spiral Stew

MAKES ABOUT 4 SERVINGS

No, this recipe does not include spiralized beef. But the inclusion of corkscrew-cut root vegetables is not only adorable, it also allows for a faster cooking time.

Ingredients

2 tablespoons flour

1 teaspoon kosher salt

½ teaspoon fresh ground black pepper

1–2 pounds beef chuck, cut in 1-inch cubes

3 tablespoons unsalted butter

1 yellow onion, minced

2 stalks celery, diced

½ teaspoon dried thyme

½ teaspoon dried oregano

2 cups red wine

2 cloves garlic, minced

1½ quarts beef stock, vegetable stock, or water

1 russet potato

2 large carrots

1 large parsnip

1 kohlrabi

3–4 large leaves kale, chopped

Additional salt and pepper as needed

2–3 tablespoons red wine vinegar

Method

1. On a shallow plate, combine flour, salt, and pepper. Rinse and pat dry the beef cubes, and roll in the seasoned flour.

2. Melt the butter in a large soup pot over medium heat. Add the onion, celery, thyme, oregano, and cook, stirring, until they become translucent. Add the floured beef to the soup pot and increase the heat to high. Cook, searing on all sides, until golden brown. Add red wine, garlic, and cover with stock or water. Stir occasionally, and when the liquid reaches a boil, reduce to a simmer, cover, and cook for 30–40 minutes, until the meat is tender and cooked through.

3. Spiralize the potato, carrots, parsnip, and kohlrabi using the straight blade to create flat spiral ribbons. Add to simmering pot, and cook until tender, about 5 minutes. Add kale and cook another 2–3 minutes. Season with salt, pepper, and red wine vinegar and serve hot with crusty bread.

(continued)

Beef Spiral Stew (continued)

More Greens: A last-minute addition of dark green leaves really ups the nutritional ante of this dish. If kale is not your thing, try it with spinach or chard instead.

Leftovers: This is a great use for leftover roast beef or steaks. After the onions and celery are translucent, whisk in a tablespoon of flour to the fat. This will make a roux to thicken the stew. Then add the diced pre-cooked meat and liquids. Bring to a boil, add the spiralized roots, then simmer for 3–5 minutes. Easy-peasy!

BBQ: If you are a BBQ fan, you can enhance this stew with your favorite sauce or spice rub. Fry some chopped bacon first and use it and the fat instead of the butter. Add your BBQ sauce or rub after the onions are translucent, than use beer instead of red wine. Finish it all with a can of kidney beans.

Chicken Soupe au Pistou with Zucchini Noodle

MAKES ABOUT 4 SERVINGS

Chicken Soup and Soupe au Pistou are technically two different things. Pistou is a French vegetable soup finished with pesto (or pistou in French). The addition of chicken is not traditional, but the flavors were born to be together. After all, fudging tradition is how great dishes are made!

Ingredients

3 tablespoons olive oil
1 yellow onion, minced
2 stalks celery, diced
1 teaspoon Herbes de Provence
2 large chicken breasts, boned, skinned, and sliced
2 cloves garlic, minced
Grated zest and juice of 1 lemon
1½ quarts chicken stock, vegetable stock, or water
2 parsnips
2 large zucchini
1 teaspoon kosher salt
½ teaspoon white pepper
¼ cup basil pesto

Method

1. Heat the oil in a large soup pot over medium heat. Add the onion, celery, herbs, and cook, stirring, until they become translucent. Add the chicken breasts and cook until browned on all sides.

2. Add the garlic, lemon zest and juice, and stock or water. When the liquid reaches a boil, reduce to a simmer, cover, and cook for 20–30 minutes, until the meat is tender and cooked through.

3. Meanwhile, spiralize the parsnips and zucchini into thin shreds using the smallest holes. Add to simmering pot, and cook until tender, about 5 minutes. Season with salt, pepper, and then serve hot topped with a dollop of pesto.

(continued)

Quick Pesto

MAKES ABOUT 1 CUP OF PESTO

There are few easier recipes than this one.

Ingredients

3 cloves garlic
½ teaspoon salt
4 cups fresh basil leaves,
    roughly chopped
¼ cup grated parmesan
    cheese
½ cup toasted pine nuts or
    walnuts
1 tablespoon lemon juice
About ¼ cup olive oil

Method

1. Using a mortar and pestle or food processor, grind the garlic and salt into a paste. Add the basil, parmesan, nuts, and lemon juice, and continue grinding. Add the oil slowly, to facilitate a paste. Season with more salt as needed. Store airtight in the refrigerator for a week, or freeze for up to several months.

> **VARIATION**
>
> **Other Birds:** This recipe is terrific with any leftover bird you might have, including chicken, turkey, game hen, or even duck. You can even use a carcass from a roasted bird, like grandma used to do. In a separate pot, cover the carcass with water and simmer for an hour or two, until the meat easily falls off the bone. Remove the carcass, cool, and pick off the meat. Use the liquid from the pot as your stock, and the meat instead of the chicken breast.

Pattypan Pho

MAKES ABOUT 4 SERVINGS

The beauty of Vietnamese pho (pronounced fuh*) is in its simplicity. Here, the use of spiralized noodles makes it easy. This recipe is grain free, but see the variation below for the addition of the traditional rice noodles. Pattypan squash are available in the summer, but if you can't find them, go ahead and use zucchini or yellow squash. In truth, it's the broth that makes this dish. This recipe speeds the process, but a rich, flavorful beef stock will help make it seem as though you worked on it all day. See page 67 for a homemade stock recipe.*

Ingredients

1 tablespoon vegetable oil

1 12–18 ounce piece of lean beef sirloin

½ teaspoon kosher salt

½ yellow onion, sliced

1 4-inch piece of ginger root, unpeeled, cut lengthwise into 4 large hunks

3 star anise pods

1 cinnamon stick

1 quart beef stock (see page 67)

4 pattypan squash

4 green onions, sliced

1–2 jalapeño chiles, sliced

1 cup mung bean sprouts

1 cup fresh cilantro leaves

¼ cup Vietnamese fish sauce

Method

1. Heat oil in a large soup pot over medium heat. Add the beef and cook each side until it is well seared, about 1 – 2 minutes per side. Beef should be charred on the outside but rare in the center. Remove from pan and set aside.

2. To the same pot add the onions, ginger, star anise, and cinnamon. Cook, stirring, until the onions just begin to color, about 2–3 minutes. Add beef stock, reduce heat, and simmer for 30 minutes.

3. Spiralize the squash into thin shreds using the smallest holes. Divide these evenly between 6 bowls. Cut the beef in thin slices against the grain, and divide between the bowls. Evenly distribute the green onions, jalapeño, mung beans, and cilantro between the bowls.

4. Remove the cinnamon stick, star anise, and ginger root from the broth. Add the fish sauce, and increase heat to high. Boil for 4–5 minutes, then ladle evenly over the ingredients in each bowl. Serve immediately.

Homemade Beef Stock

MAKES ABOUT 4 QUARTS

Proper pho broth takes several hours to make. Make this stock the next time you have beef in the house, and keep it on hand (frozen) so your pho will have an essence of authenticity. This same method can be used with chicken, veal, or pork.

Ingredients

2–3 cups leftover beef, beef bones, oxtail, or any cheap cut of meat you have on hand. (This is a great use for leftover roasts.)

1 yellow onion, diced

2 stalks celery, diced

1 large carrot, diced

1 tablespoon tomato paste

2 large tomatoes, diced

2 cups red or white wine

1 small bunch fresh thyme, stems and all

1 small bunch fresh Italian parsley, stems and all

Method

1. Preheat oven to 350°F. In a large roasting pan combine beef, onion, celery, and carrot. Roast, stirring occasionally, until the meat and vegetables are golden brown. Add tomato paste and tomatoes, and continue roasting another 10 minutes until tomatoes are browned. Add red wine and stir to deglaze the crusty bits at the bottom of the pan (what we in the business call the *fond*).

2. Transfer contents of the roasting pan to a large stockpot. Cover with cold water, place on the stove over high heat, and bring to a boil. At the boil, reduce the heat. Add the herbs, and cook at a very low simmer for 2–3 hours, skimming off any foam that appears on the surface. (In the restaurant any aromatic vegetable scraps get added to this pot as it cooks. We try to avoid extra strong flavors and colors though, such as fennel or beets. Feel free to add leftovers here as they become available.)

3. After 3 hours the liquid should be dark and flavorful. It is fine to continue simmering for a longer period if you feel the flavor isn't well developed enough. (In the restaurant business we simmer these stocks overnight.)

(continued)

Homemade Beef Stock *(continued)*

4. Strain the meat and vegetables out of the pot and discard them. Cool the stock, then refrigerate. When it is cool, the fat will rise to the surface. Scrape off and discard the fat. Your stock is now ready to use or store.

Note: There is no salt in stock because it is reduced for a long time, which intensifies the saltiness. Also, stock is usually a component of other recipes, which will be salted.

VARIATIONS

Rice Noodles: Sometimes called cellophane noodles, these clear, slippery strings are the epitome of pho. They cook in a jiffy, so add them to the broth at the very last minute. You can find them wherever Asian ingredients are sold.

Coconutty: For a real Thai twist, add a can of coconut milk (not cream of coconut, which is sweetened), to the pot at the end, and let it heat another minute before serving.

Meat Varieties: Chicken or pork also work well in this dish, as does a vegetable broth. Use what you have, and what you like!

Daikon Miso Soup with Ginger and Green Tea

MAKES ABOUT 4 SERVINGS

Miso is a Japanese seasoning paste made from fermented soybeans, and rice or barley. It is highly nutritious, containing tons of protein, vitamins, and minerals. There are several varieties, most commonly red (akamiso) or white (shiromiso), which are preferred in different regions. Generally the dark miso has been fermented longer, and therefore has a stronger, saltier flavor. It is easy to find, and easy to use. Just be sure not to let it boil. High heat kills the aroma and many of the healthful nutrients. Dashi is a broth made from bonito flakes and kombu seaweed. It is available ready-made in Asian markets, but is also easy to make yourself. See the recipe on page 70 for Homemade Dashi.

Ingredients

1 12-ounce block firm tofu

½ cup dried wakame or nori seaweed

2 tablespoons loose leaf green tea

1 4-inch piece ginger root, unpeeled, chopped roughly

1 large daikon radish

1 large carrot

1 cup dashi (store-bought or homemade, see recipe on page 70)

½ cup miso

2 green onions, chopped

1 cup edamame beans, removed from pod

Method

1. Unwrap the tofu and press it between two plates to remove some of its moisture while you prepare the broth. Use scissors to cut the wakame into thin strips. Soak in cold water for 15–30 minutes to soften and remove some of the saltiness. (Sometimes wakame can be bought precut.)

2. Bring 3 cups of water to a boil. Remove from the heat and add green tea and ginger. Steep for 15–30 minutes.

3. Cut the tofu into 1-inch cubes and set aside. Spiralize the daikon and carrot into thin shreds using the smallest holes. Set aside in a bowl of cold water.

4. Strain the tea and ginger out of the water, then bring the tea-ginger water to a boil. Add the dashi and the soaked seaweed, and cook for 4–5 minutes. Reduce the heat to a simmer, add the miso, and stir until it is well dissolved. Add the daikon, carrots, tofu, green onions, edamame, and cook until warmed through, 2–3 more minutes. Serve immediately.

(continued)

Homemade Dashi

MAKES ABOUT 2 QUARTS

Ingredients

3 4-inch pieces of kombu
  seaweed
2 cups bonito flakes

Method

1. In a large soup pot combine kombu and water and soak for 20–30 minutes, until softened.

2. Set the pot over medium heat and bring to a low simmer. When bubbles begin to appear, remove the kombu and discard. (Frugal chefs dry and reuse this kombu until there is no flavor left.) Increase the heat to high and let the liquid boil for 3–4 minutes. Reduce to a simmer, add bonito, and cook, stirring, for 10 minutes. Pass liquid though a fine mesh strainer lined with cheesecloth. Cool completely and store in the refrigerator for a week, or freeze for up to a month.

VARIATIONS

Miso: Experiment with different miso strengths.

Mushrooms: Consider an added garnish of sliced or whole mushrooms, such as the skinny enoki, the fat shitake, or the enormous eringi (aka king trumpet). Add them when the rest of the vegetables go in. You can also add dried versions, which pack a more pungent punch. Soak these first with the wakame seaweed.

Kohlrabi-Shitake Soba Noodle Soup

MAKES ABOUT 4 SERVINGS

Soba noodles are thick Japanese noodles made from buckwheat (which isn't a wheat at all, but a seed from a plant related to rhubarb). This is a great recipe if you are trying to avoid all pastas. But if you're not, and you're game to try, see the variation below using the traditional soba noodles.

Ingredients

6 cups dashi (store-bought or homemade)

6–8 pieces dried shitake mushrooms (or 1 teaspoon shitake powder)

¼ cup miso

1 teaspoon freshly grated ginger root

1 large kohlrabi

8 ounces fresh shitake mushrooms, sliced

1 teaspoon tamari or soy sauce

2 green onions

2 cups baby bok choy, thinly sliced

Shichimi chile spice blend or red chile flakes

Bonito flakes

Ponzu sauce

Method

1. In a large soup pot combine the dashi and dried shitake mushrooms. Place over high heat and bring to a boil. Reduce to a simmer and cook until mushrooms are tender, about 5 minutes. Remove mushrooms and set aside to cool.

2. Add miso and ginger to the simmering broth and stir until well dissolved.

3. Spiralize kohlrabi into thick shreds using the larger holes and add them to the simmering liquid. Slice rehydrated dry mushrooms and add them, along with the sliced fresh mushrooms, to the liquid. Add tamari, green onions, and bok choy. Simmer until warmed through. Serve warm, and offer optional toppings of shichimi, bonito, and ponzu sauce.

(continued)

Kohlrabi-Shitake Soba Noodle Soup *(continued)*

Note: Tamari and Ponzu

Tamari and Ponzu are two ubiquitous Japanese condiments.But to the uninitiated, it can be hard to tell them apart. Tamari is a Japanese version of soy sauce (fermented soy beans and wheat) but is produced from a by-product of miso production. In addition, Tamari has little to no wheat (depending on the manufacturer). Ponzu, often called citrus soy sauce, is actually made with rice wine, vinegar, bonito fish flakes, seaweed, and yuzu, a bitter orange. Some of the darker versions also contain soy sauce. These two subtle, pungent sauces have become staples in the Japanese kitchen. They are great to have on hand, but if you are not into stocking your pantry with random international ingredients, dependable soy sauce will do in a pinch.

VARIATIONS

Soba Noodles: Bring a separate pot of water to a boil. At the boil, add the soba noodles, and stir them to submerge. When they return to the boil, cook for 5 minutes. Drain off the hot water, then submerge in cold water. Gently rub off the accumulated excess starch, then drain again. Add to the soup recipe with the vegetables. (At this point you could also use them in other recipes, dress them as a salad, or add to other soup broths.)

Mushroom Medley: Try a variety of mushrooms for a fungi-licious variation!

Seafood: Any fresh seafood would be great in this soup. Consider adding cleaned and chopped shrimp, tuna, squid, or octopus. Whatever you add, be sure it is fresh!

Butternut Albondigas

MAKES ABOUT 4 SERVINGS

Albondigas are Spanish meatballs with an Arabic origin dating to the Muslim rule of Spain. The dish was imported to Spanish colonies where it took on a number of regional and cultural variations. In Mexico, it typically refers to a spicy, tomato-based meatball soup, which is more often than not fairly greasy. My remedy is this vegetable friendly version with spiralized vegetable "meatballs."

Ingredients

1 large butternut squash
1 red onion
¼ cup olive oil
1 cup pumpkin seeds
1 cup brown rice, cooked and cooled
1 8-ounce can white beans, drained and rinsed
1 teaspoon ground cumin
½ teaspoon dried coriander
Grated zest and juice of 1 lime
1 cup cilantro leaves
½ teaspoon kosher salt
¼ teaspoon freshly ground black pepper
½–1 teaspoon chile flakes, to taste

Method

FOR THE BALLS

1. Preheat oven to 375° F. Spiralize the butternut squash and the red onion into thin shreds using the smallest holes. Combine with 2 tablespoons of the olive oil in a large bowl, toss until well coated. Spread out the mixture on a baking sheet in an even layer. Sprinkle pumpkin seeds around the baking sheet evenly. Bake until the nuts are toasty and the squash is tender and just colored, about 10 minutes. Remove from oven when done, but keep the oven on.

2. In the oiled bowl combine rice, white beans, cumin, coriander, lime zest and juice. Use a fork or potato masher and smash the beans and rice into a chunky paste. Chop ½ cup of the cilantro and add. Stir in salt, pepper, and chile flakes.

3. Add the roasted squash, onions, and pumpkin seeds. Stir together so that the squash strings are bound by the rice-and-bean paste. Gather up walnut-sized bundles, roll into balls, and set on a lightly oiled baking sheet. Bake for 15–20 minutes, until they are firm and brown. Cool completely. (At this point, balls can be stored overnight in the refrigerator, or frozen for up to 2 weeks.)

1 yellow onion, roughly
   chopped

2 stalks celery, roughly
   chopped

1–2 jalapeño chiles,
   chopped

3 cloves garlic

2 large tomatoes, chopped

1 quart vegetable stock

1 large carrot

2 large zucchini

Salt and pepper to taste

FOR THE SOUP

1. Heat remaining oil in a large soup pot. Add the yellow onion, celery, jalapeño, and garlic. Cook, stirring, until the onion and celery are translucent. Add tomatoes, vegetable stock, and bring to a boil.

2. Using the single blade attachment spiralize the carrot and zucchini into flat corkscrew ribbons. Add the carrot to the pot and cook until tender, 2–3 minutes. Reduce the heat to a simmer, add the zucchini, and cook until warmed through, another 2–3 minutes. Stir in remaining cilantro. Season with salt and pepper, to taste.

3. Place 5–6 meatballs into each of 4 serving bowls. Ladle soup on top, being sure to evenly distribute the broth's ingredients.

Red Curry Soup with Summer Squash and Tofu

MAKES ABOUT 4 SERVINGS

Curry is a very individual recipe. There are hundreds of variations, and another hundred versions of each variation. This recipe calls for red curry, which is available in paste or sauce form in many markets. It is easy to make your own, though. If you are so inclined, see the recipe below.

Ingredients

1 12-ounce block firm tofu

1 tablespoon peanut or vegetable oil

1 tablespoon red curry paste

1 13-ounce can coconut milk

2 cups vegetable stock or water

1 tablespoon honey

1 tablespoon Thai fish sauce

½ red onion

1 yellow crookneck squash

2 green or yellow pattypan squash

1 zucchini squash

¼ cup fresh Thai basil leaves (or opal basil, or standard basil)

1 cup Jasmine rice, cooked (optional)

1 lime, cut in wedges

Method

1. Unwrap tofu and press between two heavy plates to remove some of its moisture while you prepare the broth. (I like to put a food can on top for a little extra weight, to facilitate the removal of moisture.)

2. Heat the oil in a large soup pot over medium heat. Add curry paste and cook, stirring, for a minute, until fragrant. Stir in coconut milk, vegetable stock, and bring to a simmer. Add honey, fish sauce, and simmer 2–3 minutes.

3. Dice tofu into 1-inch cubes, and add to broth. Spiralize the red onion and squash into thin shreds using the smallest holes, and add it to the broth. Simmer for 3–4 minutes, until warmed through. Add the basil just before serving. Serve this soup as is, or ladle it over cooked jasmine rice, with lime wedges as garnish.

Note: Summer vs. Winter Squashes

Summer squash refers to squashes that ripen in the summer, and have thin, edible skins. They include zucchini, yellow, and pattypan varieties. Winter squashes ripen in the fall, can be held through the winter, and have thicker skins that must be peeled. These include, among others, pumpkins, butternut, acorn, and kabocha squashes.

VARIATION

Winter Squash: Make this same recipe in the colder months using your favorite winter squash. Cook them a little longer in the broth, until they become tender.

Spicy Winter Squash Ramen

MAKES ABOUT 4 SERVINGS

Like pho and miso soups, the key to good ramen is the broth. Traditional ramen broth is made from pork, but our version is vegetarian. If you like, you can substitute a flavorful meat-based broth, and even add some shredded meat. (See the recipe for Homemade Beef Stock on page 68.)

Ingredients

2 teaspoons sesame oil

3 cloves garlic, minced

2 red Thai chiles, sliced lengthwise

6–8 pieces dried porcini mushrooms (or 1 tablespoon porcini powder)

4 cups vegetable stock

1 medium butternut squash, kabocha squash, or pumpkin

1 tablespoon tamari or soy sauce

1 tablespoon miso paste

3 green onions, chopped

Method

1. Heat oil in a large soup pot over medium heat. Add garlic, chiles, porcini mushrooms, and cook, stirring, until fragrant, about 1 minute. Add vegetable stock, bring to a boil, and cook for 2–3 minutes. Remove rehydrated dried mushrooms.

2. Spiralize the squash into thick shreds using the larger holes. Add to the broth and cook until tender, about 5 minutes. Reduce heat to a simmer and add tamari and miso. Simmer for another 3–5 minutes. Chop rehydrated mushrooms and add them back into the pot. Add green onions and simmer another minute. Serve immediately.

(continued)

Spicy Winter Squash Ramen *(continued)*

VARIATIONS

Tofu: For added protein, dice a block of firm tofu (pressed for 10–15 minutes to remove moisture, as is done in the recipe above for Red Curry), fry it with the garlic, and proceed with the recipe as written.

Greens: Brothy soups are a nice canvas for dark greens. Add them right at the end, just before serving, to maintain their texture and nutritional value. Try spinach, kale, chard or beet greens.

Hard Boiled Eggs: This is another favorite way to bump up the protein. Slice or quarter hard-boiled eggs, and add one to each serving bowl. Then pour the soup on top.

Spiralized Creamy Green Gazpacho

MAKES ABOUT 4 SERVINGS

Most people think of a chilled tomato soup when they think of Gazpacho. But there are actually several traditional versions of this refreshing Andalusian soup. The original, brought to the region by Arabs, was probably white. Tomatoes were added only after the New World was discovered. This green version is one of my favorites, and is wonderfully refreshing. See the variations for some other color options.

Ingredients

4 medium English or Persian cucumbers

1 white onion

1 medium green tomato or 2 tomatillos, roughly chopped

2 cloves garlic, minced

1 stalk celery, chopped

1 cup watercress or spinach leaves

1 cup cilantro leaves

Grated zest and juice of 1 lime

½ cup chopped almonds, lightly toasted

1 teaspoon ground cumin

½ teaspoon ground coriander

½ teaspoon kosher salt

½ teaspoon freshly ground black pepper

Method

1. Spiralize the cucumbers using the straight blade to create flat spiral ribbons. Set aside half of them for garnish. Spiralize the onion in the same manner.

2. In a blender combine the onions, the remaining cucumbers, tomato, garlic, and celery. Pulse the blender to create a chunky puree. Add the watercress, cilantro, lime zest and juice, and almonds. Continue to puree. Add cold water by tablespoons as needed to facilitate blending.

3. Add cumin, coriander, salt, pepper, and continue to puree. Add avocado and yogurt last, and puree to a thick soup consistency. Season with a little more salt and lime juice as needed, and adjust consistency with water as necessary. Chill soup for at least 30 minutes (or up to overnight).

(continued)

Spiralized Creamy Green Gazpacho *(continued)*

1 avocado, seeded and diced

1 cup plain yogurt

1 green onion, chopped fine

4. Divide reserved cucumbers between serving bowls, and pour chilled soup on top. Garnish with chopped green onions, and serve with crisp tortilla chips or crusty French bread.

VARIATIONS

Red Gazpacho: Replace the tomatillos and green tomato with super-ripe red tomatoes, and add 1–2 roasted red bell peppers (homemade or canned).

White Gazpacho: Known as Ajo Blanco in Spain, this delicious, garlicky version of chilled gazpacho is thickened with day-old bread. Increase the garlic to 5 cloves, replace the tomatoes and tomatillos with 3 cups of crustless cubed day-old bread (sourdough is great here), and a cup of dried and plumped golden raisins or figs. Omit the green herbs and avocado, flavor with dry Spanish sherry, and garnish with a drizzle of great olive oil.

Thom Kha Gai

MAKES ABOUT 4 SERVINGS

This classic Thai soup is frequently made with chicken. Again, this is a vegetarian version, but you can easily add chunks of cooked chicken breast and a flavorful chicken stock. The more unusual ingredients can be found in most Asian markets, but can also be replaced easily by more domestic ingredients in a pinch.

Ingredients

1 4-inch piece ginger root
1 stalk lemon grass (or
    grated zest of 3 lemons)
5 makrut lime leaves (or
    grated zest of 3 limes)
6 cups vegetable stock
2 sweet potatoes
2 cups oyster or shitake
    mushrooms, roughly
    chopped
1 13-ounce can coconut milk
2 tablespoons Thai fish
    sauce
1 teaspoon honey
1 cup cilantro leaves, whole
1 lime, cut into wedges
Thai chili oil

Method

1. Roughly chop the ginger, lemon grass, and makrut lime leaves. Combine them with vegetable stock in a large soup pot and bring to a boil over high heat. Reduce to a simmer and cook for 30 minutes. Use a slotted spoon or strainer to remove ginger, lemon grass, and makrut lime leaves.

2. Spiralize sweet potatoes into thin shreds using the smallest holes and add them to the broth, along with the mushrooms. Simmer until the sweet potatoes are tender, about 5 minutes.

3. Stir in coconut milk, fish sauce, and honey, and simmer another 2–3 minutes. Add the cilantro just before serving. Offer lime wedges and chili oil to your guests to add as they please.

VARIATION

Protein: This soup is the perfect place to use a little leftover chicken, beef, pork, or fish. Add it, precooked, to the broth in the early stages. Add diced firm tofu (pressed for 15 minutes to remove excess moisture, as described in the Red Curry recipe on page 76) with the sweet potatoes at the end, and let simmer to warm through.

Vegetable Minestrone

MAKES ABOUT 6 SERVINGS

Minestrone is classic peasant food with origins that predate the Roman Republic. This classic Italian soup was vegetarian by necessity, with the protein content bulked up with beans and pasta or rice. This version is vegetarian by choice, including the vegetable "pasta." You can, however, add noodles if you are a traditionalist. Pasta or not, the key to a great minestrone is good caramelization of the vegetables before the liquid is added.

Ingredients

2 tablespoons olive oil
1 yellow onion, diced
2 stalks celery, diced
2 cloves garlic
1 tablespoon dried oregano
1 tablespoon dried basil
1 teaspoon dried thyme
1 cup red wine
1 14-ounce can crushed
   tomatoes
1 tablespoon tomato paste
5 cups vegetable stock or
   water
1 large carrot
1 parsnip
1 celery root
1 zucchini squash
1 8-ounce can kidney beans
1 8-ounce can white beans

(continued)

Method

1. Heat oil in a large soup pot over medium heat. Add onions and celery and cook, stirring, until they are tender and caramelized, about 3–5 minutes. Add the garlic, oregano, basil, thyme, and cook another minute until the garlic just begins to color. Add red wine, bring to a boil, and cook until reduced by half, about 3–5 minutes. Stir in the tomatoes and tomato paste.

2. Add the stock and bring to a boil. At the boil, reduce heat to a simmer and cook 30 minutes to concentrate flavors. Spiralize carrot, parsnip, and celery root using the straight blade to create flat spiral ribbons. Add them to the simmering pot, and cook until tender, about 5 minutes. Spiralize zucchini and set aside.

3. Add the beans, salt, pepper, and vinegar to season. Add zucchini just before serving and cook another 1–2 minutes to warm through. Garnish with a sprinkling of chopped fresh basil and parmesan cheese.

(continued)

Vegetable Minestrone *(continued)*

1 teaspoon kosher salt

½ teaspoon fresh ground black pepper

2–3 tablespoon red wine vinegar, as needed

¼ cup fresh basil leaves, chopped

¼ cup freshly grated parmesan cheese

VARIATIONS

Extra Veggies: This is traditionally a "leftovers" soup, so feel free to add in your veggie leftovers. Nothing is off limits—green beans, broccoli, cauliflower, eggplant, leafy greens—whatever you have on hand.

Real Noodles: Adding dry pasta to this recipe will thicken the broth considerably. (It will turn out more like a stew). To combat this, you can add extra water, or precook the noodles separately and add them at the end, with the zucchini.

zoodles
(zucchini noodles)

*Why a whole chapter on zucchini?
Because they are by far the easiest and
most popular food to spiralize.*

Browned Butter Zucchini Späetzle

MAKES 2 SERVINGS

The word Späetzle *means "little sparrow," although how these little egg noodle nuggets came to be named after a bird is a mystery. These little noodles are thought to have originated in Southern Germany during the Middle Ages. Here, the name is nothing but an homage, pairing our späetzlized squash with the traditional brown butter sauce.*

Ingredients

¼ cup unsalted butter
2 large zucchini squash
½ teaspoon kosher salt
¼ cup freshly grated
   parmesan cheese

Method

1. Melt the butter in a large sauté pan over medium heat. When it is completely melted, and the bubbles subside, continue to let it cook. The solids will fall to the bottom of the pan and toast. Let them get brown, and then black, then remove the pan from the heat and set aside. It might smoke a bit, which is okay. The black bits are essential to this dish's nutty flavor.

2. Meanwhile, spiralize the zucchini into thick shreds using the larger holes. Chop them into 1-inch lengths. Add them to the browned butter with the salt, return the pan to the heat and toss until just warmed through. Serve immediately with a sprinkling of parmesan cheese.

VARIATION

Veggie Options: Potatoes and sweet potatoes make a great version of this dish. Because they take a little longer to cook than zucchini, cook them in boiling water for 3–5 minutes before adding them to the browned butter. Try the same with other winter squashes.

Roasted Shrimp with Garlic-Zucchini Fettuccini

MAKES 2 LARGE SERVINGS

How can a dish this easy make people so happy?

Ingredients

1 pound of medium shrimp, shelled, deveined, and cleaned

2–4 tablespoons extra virgin or regular olive oil

4 roma tomatoes, quartered lengthwise

1 red onion, chopped into wedges

½ teaspoon dried thyme

3 large zucchini

4 cloves garlic

½ teaspoon salt

¼ cup fresh Italian parsley leaves, chopped

¼ cup freshly grated parmesan cheese

Method

1. Preheat oven to 375°F. Combine shrimp, 2 tablespoons olive oil, tomatoes, onion, thyme, and toss together to coat well with oil. Spread onto a baking sheet and roast until the shrimp are pink. Using tongs, quickly remove shrimp and return the pan of tomatoes and onions to the oven. Keep shrimp warm. Continue roasting until the tomatoes are charred and the onion is well caramelized.

2. Spiralize the zucchini into thick shreds using the larger holes. Heat 2 tablespoons of oil in a large sauté pan over medium heat. Add garlic, reduce heat, and cook slowly until translucent.

3. Add zucchini and toss to warm through. Add shrimp, tomatoes, onions, salt, and toss to coat with garlic oil. Divide between serving plates, and garnish each with a sprinkle of chopped parsley and parmesan cheese.

> **VARIATIONS**
>
> **Shrimpless:** If you have vegan tendencies, feel free to omit the shrimp and add a few more tomatoes. And consider some colorful heirloom varieties. Golden and green tomatoes are delicious and beautiful!

Zucchini with Sweet Roasted Kale and Red Onions

MAKES 2 LARGE SERVINGS

There are two kinds of kale generally available in the market. One is curly, which is generally too fibrous for salads, and the other is Tuscan or dinosaur kale, which is preferable for this recipe. Baby kale is also available occasionally, which is the bomb if you can find it!

Ingredients

6–8 large kale leaves, stems removed

1 red onion

3–4 tablespoons olive oil regular

1 cup sliced almonds

3 large zucchini squash

1 clove garlic

Grated zest and juice of 1 orange

1 tablespoon honey

1 tablespoon balsamic vinegar

½ teaspoon kosher salt

½ teaspoon white pepper as is

¼ teaspoon or more red chile flakes

Method

1. Preheat oven to 375°F. Roughly chop the kale, spiralize the onion into thin shreds using the smallest holes, and combine them in a large bowl with 1 tablespoon of olive oil until well-coated. Spread onto a baking sheet and roast until the leaves are charred and the onions begin to brown. Spread almonds onto a second baking pan and toast in the same oven until fragrant and golden, about 5–10 minutes.

2. Spiralize zucchini into thin shreds using the smallest holes. Set aside. Heat 2 tablespoons of olive oil in a large saucepan over medium heat. Add garlic and cook until softened. Stir in orange zest and juice, honey, vinegar, salt, pepper and chile flakes. Add zucchini and cook, tossing to coat, until just tender, about 2 minutes. Toss in kale and onion just before serving with a garnish of toasted almonds.

Spiralized Vegetable Lasagna

MAKES ABOUT 4 TO 6 SERVINGS

Until the spiralizer came along there was nothing new under the sun in the land of lasagna. But these corkscrew-cut vegetables provide more spaces for the luscious sauce and cheeses to nestle. Definitely a leap forward in lasagna technology.

Ingredients

3 large, very firm Japanese
   eggplant
2 tablespoons kosher salt,
2–4 tablespoons olive oil
1 red onion, diced
3 cloves garlic
1 teaspoon dried oregano
1 teaspoon dried basil
½ teaspoon dried thyme
1 cup red wine
1 8-ounce can tomatoes
1 tablespoon tomato paste
Kosher salt and freshly
   ground black pepper, to
   taste

Method

1. Spiralize the eggplant using the straight blade to create flat spiral ribbons. Toss with the salt to coat evenly, place in a colander, and set aside at room temperature. The salt will leach out the moisture, reduce the bitterness, and make the eggplant more flavor absorbent. (See page 10 for information about spiralizing eggplant.)

2. Heat 1 tablespoon of oil in a large saucepan over medium heat. Add the red onion and cook, stirring, until they begin to caramelize. Add garlic, dried herbs, and cook another minute. Add wine and cook, stirring, until the liquid is reduced by half. Add tomatoes, tomato paste, and simmer for 20–30 minutes. Remove from heat, season with salt and pepper, and set aside to cool.

3. Heat 1 tablespoon of oil in a large sauté pan. Add half the yellow onion, and cook until translucent. Add mushrooms and a pinch of salt. Cook until the mushrooms are browned. Transfer sautéed mushrooms to a plate to cool and return the pan to the stove.

1 yellow onion, diced

8 ounces crimini or button mushrooms, sliced

4 cups baby spinach leaves

2 large zucchini

2 yellow squash

1 bulb fennel

8 ounces ricotta cheese

8 ounces fresh mozzarella (buffalo)

½ cup freshly grated parmesan cheese

4. Heat another tablespoon of oil, add the remaining onion, and cook until the onion begins to caramelize. Add the spinach and a pinch of salt. Cook, tossing, until the spinach is wilted. Remove from heat and set aside to cool.

5. Rinse the salt off the eggplant and pat dry. Spiralize the zucchini, yellow squash, and fennel using the straight blade to create flat spiral ribbons. Preheat oven to 375°F.

6. In a large baking dish begin layering the lasagna in the following order: tomato sauce, zucchini, fennel, spinach, ricotta, eggplant, mushrooms, mozzarella. Repeat this pattern, doing your best to distribute the ingredients evenly across each layer. Finish with sauce and a sprinkling of parmesan cheese. Cover the dish and bake until it begins to bubble, about 30 minutes. Remove cover and cook an additional 5–10 minutes to brown the top and evaporate any accumulated liquid. Serve hot.

VARIATION

Meaty Lasagna: You can add meat easily to this recipe. Choose Italian sausage or ground beef and add it in the beginning of the sauce preparation, browning it in the oil before the onions are added. Alternatively, you can layer your ingredients with already cooked ground beef, sausage, roasted turkey, or chicken.

Moroccan Zucchini with Cauliflower-Couscous Meatballs

MAKES ABOUT 2 LARGE SERVINGS

Moroccan cuisine, like much of the ancient foods touched by Arab influence and Silk Road spice traders, is exotically aromatic. The combination here of sweet and savory spices is typical of that region. The spiralizer is not.

Ingredients

½ head cauliflower, chopped roughly

4 cloves garlic

2–4 tablespoons olive oil

1 cup couscous

½ teaspoon kosher salt

½ teaspoon freshly ground black pepper

½ teaspoon cinnamon

1 teaspoon cumin

1 teaspoon ground cardamom

½ teaspoon ground anise seeds

Grated zest and juice of 1 lime

3 large zucchini

¼ cup freshly grated parmesan cheese

Method

1. Preheat oven to 375°F. Toss cauliflower and whole peeled garlic cloves in olive oil, and spread out in a single layer on a baking sheet. Roast until the cauliflower is golden and the garlic is fragrant. Cool to room temperature. (Keep the oven on.)

2. Meanwhile, combine couscous and water in a small saucepan over high heat. Bring to a boil, then reduce heat to low, cover, and simmer for 10 minutes. Turn off the heat and set aside until the water is absorbed. Cool to room temperature.

3. Process or chop the cauliflower and garlic until it resembles a paste. Transfer to a large bowl and add the cooled couscous, salt, and pepper. In a separate bowl, combine the cinnamon, cumin, cardamom and anise. Add half to the cauliflower mixture, along with lime zest and juice. Slowly drizzle in olive oil and stir until the mixture holds together.

4. Roll the cauliflower mixture into walnut-sized balls, and set on a lightly oiled baking sheet. Bake for 10–20 minutes, until they are golden brown.

(continued)

5. Spiralize zucchini into thin shreds using the smallest holes. Heat a tablespoon of oil in a large sauté pan. Add the remaining spice mix, the zucchini, and a pinch of salt. Cook, tossing, until tender, about 2 minutes. Add cauliflower balls and toss to coat, then serve immediately. Garnish with a sprinkling of parmesan cheese.

VARIATION

Harissa: If you like heat, try a dash or two of harissa. This North African hot chile condiment would make a great finish to this dish. (See the recipe for homemade harissa on page 119.)

Zucchini Pasta with Puttanesca Sauce

MAKES ABOUT 2 SERVINGS

This salty dish is named for the Italian ladies of the night, who either made this dish frequently to entice customers, or because its ingredients are all precooked and canned, making the dish easy to whip up in between . . . er . . . jobs.

Ingredients

3 large zucchini squash
2 tablespoons olive oil
2 cloves garlic, minced
1 2-ounce can anchovy
   filets, roughly chopped
1 cup kalamata olives, pitted and roughly chopped
1 tablespoon capers
1 12-ounce can crushed
   tomatoes
¼ cup fresh basil leaves, cut
   in chiffonade

Method

1. Spiralize zucchini into thick shreds using the larger holes. Set aside.

2. Heat olive oil in a large sauté pan over medium heat. Add garlic and cook until barely brown, about 1 minute. Add anchovies, olives, capers, and cook, stirring, for 1 minute.

3. Add tomatoes and bring to a boil. Reduce heat and simmer for 5 minutes. Add zucchini and cook, tossing to coat zucchini with sauce, until tender. Serve hot sprinkled with chiffonade of basil.

Herbed Zucchini with Walnut Pesto

MAKES ABOUT 2 SERVINGS

The term pesto *is a reference to this sauce's preparation—made with a mortar and pestle. It does not have to contain basil. Here, the main flavor comes from toasted nuts. Pulverizing them while warm takes advantage of the natural nut oils. There is basil here, but you can easily use any other fresh herb you might have on hand. Try with pistachios, pecans, almonds, hazelnuts, or the traditional pine nut.*

Ingredients

2 cups walnuts
2 cloves garlic
¼ cup fresh mint leaves
¼ cup fresh basil leaves
2 green onions, chopped
½ teaspoon kosher salt
2–4 tablespoons olive oil
3 large zucchini
¼ cup freshly grated
    parmesan cheese

Method

1. Preheat oven to 350°F. Spread walnuts in a single layer on a baking sheet, and toast until they become brown and fragrant.

2. While the walnuts are still warm, transfer them to a food processor or blender and grind into a paste. Add garlic, mint, basil, green onions, and salt. Continue to process, adding oil slowly, as necessary, until the mixture reaches a smooth pesto texture.

3. Spiralize zucchini into thin shreds using the smallest holes. Heat a tablespoon of olive oil in a large sauté pan over medium heat. Add zucchini and cook, tossing in the oil, until tender, about 1–2 minutes. Add pesto, and toss together to coat well. Serve warm, garnished with a sprinkle of parmesan cheese and walnuts.

Note: Try this with mint only, or add Italian parsley, delicate chervil, or peppery watercress.

Zucchini Carbonara

MAKES ABOUT 2 SERVINGS

This dish is thought to represent the traditional lunch of Italian coal miners. Whether or not that's true, it is for sure an easy and delicious recipe. Be sure to add the egg off the heat, or you will end up with Zucchini in Scrambled Egg Sauce.

Ingredients

2 eggs

1 cup heavy cream

1 cup freshly grated parmesan cheese

4 ounces pancetta or bacon, diced

½ yellow onion, diced

3 cloves garlic, minced

¼ teaspoon kosher salt

½ teaspoon freshly ground black pepper

3 large zucchini squash

¼ cup Italian parsley leaves, chopped

Method

1. In a small bowl whisk together eggs, cream, and ¾ cup of the parmesan cheese, and set aside.

2. Place a large sauté pan over medium heat, add the pancetta, and cook until the fat is rendered and the meat is crisp. Remove the meat from the fat and set aside. Add the onion to the fat and cook until it browns. Add garlic and cook just until it softens. Add salt and pepper.

3. Meanwhile, spiralize the zucchini into thick shreds using the larger holes. When the garlic is soft, add the zucchini and toss to coat with fat and cook until warmed through, about 2–3 minutes. Turn off the heat, add the cream and egg mixture, and toss it quickly to coat everything evenly. Serve immediately, sprinkled with remaining parmesan and chopped parsley.

> **VARIATION**
>
> **Meatless:** Carbonara has meat by definition, but here is a vegetarian version. Use 2 tablespoons olive oil instead of the pancetta. You can leave it at that, or add a ½ cup of chopped mushrooms with the onions and garlic

Zucchini with Lentil Bolognese

MAKES ABOUT 4 SERVINGS

Bolognese is the traditional tomato-based sauce from Bologna, Italy, made classically with slow braised beef. Here, I offer you a vegetarian version, using lentils. For those with a hankering for the original, see the variations below.

Ingredients

2 tablespoons olive oil

1 yellow onion, diced

2 stalks celery, diced

1 large carrot, diced

½ teaspoon dried oregano

½ teaspoon dried basil

¼ teaspoon dried thyme

6 cloves garlic, minced

2 cups green lentils, rinsed

4 cups vegetable stock or water

1 12-ounce can crushed tomatoes

2 tablespoons tomato paste

½ teaspoon kosher salt

½ teaspoon freshly ground black pepper

4 large zucchini squash

¼ cup fresh Italian parsley leaves, chopped

¼ cup freshly grated parmesan cheese

Method

1. Heat oil in a large sauté pan over medium heat. Add onion, celery, carrot, herbs, and half of the garlic. Cook until they begin to brown, about 2 minutes. Add lentils, and cook, stirring for 1 minute. Add stock and bring to a boil. Reduce heat and simmer until lentils are tender, about 30 minutes.

2. Add tomatoes, tomato paste, bring back to a simmer, and cook another 10–15 minutes. Season with salt and pepper.

3. Spiralize zucchini into thin shreds using the smallest holes. Heat 2 tablespoons of oil in a large sauté pan. Add remaining garlic and zucchini, a pinch of salt, and cook, tossing to coat with oil, until tender, about 2–3 minutes. Serve bowls of zucchini topped with a ladle of lentil Bolognese and a sprinkle of chopped parsley and parmesan cheese.

(continued)

Zucchini with Lentil Bolognese *(continued)*

VARIATION

Alternative Bean: Lentils produce a texture similar to ground beef. The same can be achieved by smashing up larger beans. Try it with white beans, garbanzos, or kidney beans instead. If you use precooked canned beans, reduce the cooking time.

Traditional Bolognese: Instead of lentils, add to the pot of vegetables some lesser cuts of meat with a lot of marbling and connective tissue (such as chuck or shanks). Cover with water and simmer slowly for 60 – 90 minutes, until the meat is tender, and falls apart easily. Remove the meat from the pot, cool slightly, mince, then add back to the pot. Continue with the recipe as written. Adjust seasoning as necessary.

Zucchini Primavera

MAKES ABOUT 2 SERVINGS

Primavera is French for spring, and this recipe features baby spring vegetables. You can, however, make this any time of year using the adult versions of these veggies. Cut them small, and be careful not to overcook them.

Ingredients

3 large zucchini squash
2 tablespoons olive oil
3 green onions, chopped
1 tablespoon fresh thyme
    leaves
6–8 baby carrots, peeled
    and halved lengthwise
4 baby zucchini squash,
    halved lengthwise
4 baby yellow squash,
    halved lengthwise
1 cup fresh baby peas
1 cup heavy cream
¼ teaspoon kosher salt
¼ teaspoon white pepper
¼ cup Italian parsley
    leaves, chopped

Method

1. Spiralize zucchini into thin shreds using the smallest holes. Set aside.

2. Heat oil in a large sauté pan over medium heat. Add the green onions, thyme and cook, stirring until translucent. Add carrots, water, reduce heat to a simmer, and cook until carrots are tender.

3. Add the baby squash and continue cooking until tender and golden. Add peas, cream, salt, pepper, and simmer to reduce cream by half.

4. Add zucchini and cook, tossing to coat zucchini with sauce, until tender, about 2–3 minutes. Serve hot sprinkled with chopped parsley.

main events

The recipes in this chapter use a variety of vegetables to create hearty, entrée-worthy dishes. And although the standard use of the spiralizer is to make vegetable "pasta," I have discovered that the options are by no means limited to traditional pasta dishes. Prepare to have your mind blown.

Butternut Squash and Pecorino Risotto

MAKES ABOUT 4 SERVINGS

Butternut squash is not inclined to hold a long "noodle" shape. This rebellious winter squash might start out long, but it slowly breaks apart into smaller and smaller pieces the more it is handled. This phenomenon, as it turns out, makes it perfect to replace rice.

Ingredients

½ cup pine nuts

1 large butternut squash

2 tablespoons olive oil, extra virgin or regular

2 cloves garlic, sliced

1 teaspoon fresh thyme leaves

½ teaspoon Herbes de Provence

1 cup vegetable stock or water

¾ cup freshly grated pecorino cheese

½ teaspoon kosher salt

½ teaspoon freshly ground black pepper

Method

1. Preheat oven to 350°F. Spread pine nuts onto a baking sheet and bake until toasted and fragrant, about 10 minutes. Cool.

2. Spiralize butternut squash into thin shreds using the smallest holes. Break the strands into pieces about 1 inch long, either by hand, or with a knife. Set aside.

3. Heat oil in a large saucepan. Add garlic, thyme, Herbes de Provence, and cook until garlic is translucent. Add squash and toss to coat. Add stock and simmer, stirring, until squash is tender and liquid is evaporated, about 3–5 minutes.

4. Stir in ½ cup of pecorino, and season with salt and pepper. Serve hot topped with a sprinkle of toasted pine nuts and the remaining ¼ cup of pecorino cheese.

VARIATION

Veggie Variety: This same recipe can be made with any number of root vegetables. Try it with sweet potatoes, celery root, yucca, or rutabaga. The harder ones, like parsnips or carrots, will get "rice-ier" if you pulse the spiralized strings briefly in a food processor.

Curried Cauliflower, Cabbage, and White Bean Hamburger Patties

These patties are 100 times better than any premade, processed vegetable burger you can buy in the market. I love the addition of curry, but if you're looking for a more traditionally flavored patty, see the variations. Many incarnations of curry powder are readily available. But you can make your own flavorful blend easily at home. See the recipe on page 115.

Ingredients

1 head cauliflower

1 russet potato

1 head savoy cabbage

1 yellow onion

2–4 tablespoons olive oil

1 8-ounce can white beans, drained

1 egg

2–4 tablespoons curry powder

Method

1. Preheat oven to 375°F. Chop the cauliflower roughly into small pieces. Spiralize the potato, cabbage, and onion into thin shreds using the smallest holes. Combine in a large bowl and toss with 1–2 tablespoons of olive oil. Spread out onto a baking sheet and roast until golden brown and tender, about 10–15 minutes. Cool.

2. Place drained beans in a large bowl and mash roughly with a spoon. Add the egg, curry powder, and mix thoroughly. Chop the roasted cauliflower mixture into smaller minced pieces, then add them to the bowl. Stir the mixture into a paste. Gather up ¼–½ cup of paste and form into patties. Chill patties for 15–30 minutes.

(continued)

3. Heat 1–2 tablespoons of oil in a large saucepan over medium heat. Cook patties in batches until golden brown, about 3–5 minutes on each side. Be careful not to crowd them in the pan. Serve warm, or cool and store for later use. They will keep in the refrigerator for 2 days, or in the freezer for up to two weeks.

Note: *Curry Blends*

There are different blends of curry in every different region of the Far East. They are easy to make and much more delicious than the pre-ground, pre-blended variety. Use a coffee grinder for best results. (I have one grinder designated as a spice-only grinder. That way, my coffee doesn't taste weird.)

VARIATIONS

Pesto Burgers: Replace the curry powder with ¼ cup or more of your favorite pesto.

Mexi-Burgers: Replace the white beans with black beans, and the curry powder with a tablespoon of cumin, ½ teaspoon of coriander, 1 chopped jalapeño, and ¼ cup of chopped fresh cilantro. Alternatively you can add ¼ cup of your favorite premade salsa.

Curry Powder Blend (Garam Masala)

MAKES ABOUT ¾ TO 1 CUP OF CURRY POWDER

Garam means "warm" or "hot," but not spicy-hot. The name may refer to the toasting of the seeds prior to grinding, or the warm feeling you get after eating it.

Ingredients

1 cup bay leaf

½ cup cumin seed

¼ cup coriander seed

3 tablespoons freshly ground black pepper

3 tablespoons cardamom seed

3 tablespoons whole clove

1 whole nutmeg, crushed

Method

1. Combine all the spices in a bowl. Toast them in a dry skillet until fragrant (but not burned) before grinding to a fine powder in a mortar or coffee grinder.

VARIATIONS

Chaat Masala: Chaat means "to lick," which is what you will do to your lips after eating this blend. Use the same recipe as above, omitting the coriander, and adding to the blend a few more exotic spices, which can be found in Indian markets. Add a tablespoon each of amchoor, cubeb pepper, ajwain, asafetida, fresh mint, and ginger.

Char Masala: This is a simple toasted blend. Use the method above with 2 tablespoons cumin, 1 tablespoon cardamom, 1 teaspoon allspice, and 1 crushed cinnamon stick.

Harissa Rutabaga with Kale, Chick Peas, and Poached Egg

MAKES 4 TO 6 SERVINGS

Harissa is essentially a spicy Magrebian pesto. The national condiment of Tunisia, it is also used extensively in the cuisines of Morocco, Algeria, and has found its way into the foods of the Middle East. You can find ready-made harissa paste, but if you have time and the inclination, it's fun to make it yourself. (See recipe on page 119.) Za'atar, used as garnish in this dish, is a popular spice blend used throughout North Africa and the Middle East. If you can't find it feel free to simply use some freshly ground black pepper.

Ingredients

3 large rutabagas
2–4 tablespoons olive oil
1 head black kale leaves
1 teaspoon white wine
   vinegar
4–6 eggs
1 8-ounce can chickpeas
   (aka garbanzo beans),
   drained
2 tablespoons harissa
¼ cup fresh mint leaves
¼ cup fresh basil leaves
¼ teaspoon kosher salt
Grated zest and juice of
   1 lemon
1 teaspoon za'atar
¼ cup shelled peanuts,
   chopped

Method

1. Preheat oven to 350°F. Spiralize the rutabaga into thick shreds using the larger holes. Toss with 1 tablespoon oil to coat evenly. Spread onto a baking sheet and roast until toasted, about 5 minutes. Set aside, and keep warm.

2. Remove the stem from the kale leaves and chop the leaves roughly. Toss in 1 teaspoon of oil, then spread onto a baking sheet and roast until golden and tender, about 10–15 minutes. Set aside.

3. Bring a small saucepan of water with vinegar to a boil. Crack 1 egg in a small dish, being careful not to break the yolk. Turn the heat down to a simmer, stir the pot of water to create a gentle whirlpool, then slowly drop the egg in the center. Cook gently, until the white is solidified. Remove from the water with a slotted spoon, and transfer to a bowl of cold water. Repeat with remaining eggs. Keep the pot of warm water on a low simmer.

(continued)

Harissa Rutabaga *(continued)*

4. Heat 1 tablespoon of oil in a large sauté pan. Add chickpeas and sauté, shaking the pan, until browned. Add harissa and toss to coat and warm through. Add rutabaga, kale, mint, basil, and lemon zest, tossing to coat. Season with salt and lemon juice, then divide between serving plates.

5. Remove poached eggs from the cold water and resubmerge in the simmering water for 20–30 seconds to warm through. Remove each with the slotted spoon, blot on a paper towel, and place one egg on top of each plate. Serve immediately, garnished with za'atar and chopped peanuts.

VARIATION

Meaty: If you are not avoiding meat, try making this dish with the addition of lamb, beef, or chicken. Use precooked (preferably leftover) meats, cut into bite-sized bits, and sauté them with the chickpeas.

Harissa

MAKES ABOUT 1 TO 1½ CUPS OF HARISSA

I use my preferred dried chiles in this recipe, but you can certainly use any other dried chile or mix of chiles that you have on hand.

Ingredients

4 dried guajillo chiles,
4 dried New Mexico chiles
¼ teaspoon cumin seeds
¼ teaspoon coriander seeds
¼ teaspoon caraway seeds
6–8 fresh mint leaves
4 cloves garlic
Grated zest and juice of
   1 lemon
½ teaspoon kosher salt
2–4 tablespoons olive oil

Method

1. Toast chiles on a griddle, or in the oven, until crisp and fragrant, about 1–2 minutes, turning them frequently. Cool completely, then remove the stems and seeds. (Consider using gloves, as the capsicum will adhere to your hands and spread with your touch.) Cover stemmed and seeded chiles in boiling water and set aside to soften for 15–20 minutes.

2. Toast spices in a hot, dry skillet. Keep them moving until they become fragrant, about 1 minute. Transfer to a coffee grinder and pulverize to a powder.

3. Drain the chiles and combine them with mint, garlic, lemon zest and juice, ground spices, and salt in a food processor or mortar. Puree into a smooth paste, adding olive oil as needed until the desired consistency is reached. Store in the refrigerator, with a thin layer of olive oil on the surface.

Parsnip and Celery Root Pasta with Roasted Garlic and Pine Nuts

MAKES ABOUT 2 SERVINGS

This recipe features two of my favorite underappreciated vegetables, and my favorite use of garlic. I'm confident that once you try this you'll agree.

Ingredients

2 whole bulbs of garlic

2–4 tablespoons olive oil, extra virgin or regular

1 cup pine nuts

3 parsnips, peeled

1 celery root, peeled

1 tablespoon fresh thyme leaves

½ teaspoon kosher salt

½ teaspoon freshly ground black pepper

2 cups heavy cream

1–2 tablespoons freshly squeezed lemon juice

½ cup shaved manchego cheese (or other firm cheese)

Method

1. Preheat oven to 400°F. Coat garlic bulbs lightly in oil, wrap in foil, and bake until tender, about 30 minutes. Meanwhile, spread pine nuts onto a baking sheet and toast in the oven as well, until golden brown and fragrant, about 5–8 minutes. Cool both.

2. Spiralize parsnips and celery root into thin shreds using the smallest holes. Set aside.

3. Heat 2 tablespoons of oil in a large sauté pan. Cut the root end off of each roasted garlic bulb, and squeeze the roasted garlic paste into the pan. Add thyme, salt, pepper, cream, and whisk to combine. Add the parsnips and celery root, toss to coat evenly with sauce, and simmer until the cream is thickened and the roots are tender, about 3–5 minutes. Serve immediately topped with a squeeze of lemon juice and a sprinkle of grated manchego cheese.

Artichokes: The addition of artichoke hearts (canned in water, not in oil) adds a unique umami quality to this already unique dish. Sautéed sunchokes (aka Jerusalem artichokes) give a similar effect.

Olives: The addition of chopped kalamata olives gives this dish a lip-smacking tang.

Potato Pizza

This is a favorite of the gluten-shy. Be warned that white potatoes pack a lot of carbs, so if it's the carbs you are avoiding, consider making this recipe with sweet potatoes, which have more nutrients, and a lower glycemic index.

Ingredients

2 large russet potatoes
½ teaspoon kosher salt
2–4 tablespoons vegetable oil
½ cup pesto sauce (See page 65)
1 large heirloom or vine-ripened tomato, sliced
8 ounces fresh mozzarella, thinly sliced
2 cloves garlic, sliced
½ cup fresh basil leaves, chopped
2–4 tablespoons olive oil, extra virgin if possible

Method

1. Spiralize potatoes into thin shreds using the smallest holes. Toss with salt and set aside.

2. Heat 2 tablespoons of oil in a large sauté pan over high heat. Gather the potato noodles and place them all in the hot oiled pan. (Be careful, the oil might splatter.) Press them into a flat cake, and cook on high heat for 1–2 minutes. Shake pan occasionally to keep from sticking. Reduce heat and cook until the bottom is golden brown and set. Flip and repeat on the other side. Add another tablespoon or two of oil if necessary. When golden on both sides, transfer from sauté pan to a lightly oiled baking sheet. This is your pizza "crust."

3. Preheat oven to 375°F. Spread pesto sauce evenly across the top of the potato crust. Arrange tomato slices, evenly across the pesto, and repeat with the mozzarella. Sprinkle sliced garlic all over, then drizzle the surface with olive oil.

(continued)

Potato Pizza *(continued)*

4. Bake pizza for 10–20 minutes, until the cheese is melted and the toppings are bubbling. Remove from oven and top with basil. Slice in wedges and serve immediately.

VARIATION

Pizza Jardiniere: For a fresh, garden-style pizza, top the potatoes with an assortment of fresh greens, lemon zest, olive oil, garlic, and salt. Bake until the greens begin to wilt.

Pumpkin Mac and Cheese

MAKES ABOUT 2 SERVINGS

The key to this dish is mise en place, *the French term for "putting in place." It refers to getting all your equipment and ingredients ready before you start a recipe. The cheese sauce for this dish, which is essentially béchamel sauce, needs your undivided attention.*

Ingredients

1 medium pumpkin, peeled, seeded, and cut into large chunks

3 tablespoons butter

1 yellow onion, diced fine

1 teaspoon dried thyme

2 tablespoons whole wheat flour (any gluten-free flour is fine, too)

1 cup milk (plain almond or soy milks are fine here, too)

1 teaspoon Dijon mustard

¼ teaspoon freshly grated nutmeg

1 cup sharp white cheddar cheese

¼ cup grated parmesan cheese

½ teaspoon kosher salt

½ teaspoon freshly ground black pepper

Method

1. Preheat oven to 375°F. Spiralize pumpkin into thick shreds using the largest holes. Break the strands into pieces about 1 inch long, either by hand, or with a knife. Set aside.

2. Bring a pot of water to a boil over high heat. Add pumpkin and cook until tender, about 2–3 minutes. Drain and set aside in the colander to continue draining as it cools.

3. Melt butter in a large sauté pan over medium heat. Add onions, thyme, and cook until they just begin to brown. Whisk in flour to make a roux. (The mixture will quickly thicken into a paste.) Slowly drizzle in milk, stirring, until a thick white sauce is created. (If it still seems too thick for you, continue to slowly add more milk until desired consistency is reached.) Remove from heat and stir in mustard, nutmeg, and grated cheese. Season with salt and pepper.

4. Fold cooked pumpkin into cheese sauce, and transfer to a baking dish. Top with parmesan cheese and bake, uncovered, until brown and bubbly, about 20 minutes.

(continued)

Pumpkin Mac and Cheese *(continued)*

VARIATIONS

Cheese Options: There are so many cheeses that make great Mac. Stay away from the stringier varieties, such as jack and mozzarella. But do try any cheddar, fontina, muenster—or make a blend. And don't overlook the pungent cheeses! Goats and blues are quite delicious here!

Protein Additions: This dish is great with an added handful or two of diced smoky ham, chorizo or andouille sausage, succulent lobster, shrimp, or crab. Stir in to the cheese sauce just before you add the pumpkin.

Truffles: The addition of truffles (the fungi, not the chocolate bonbons) or truffle oil is a popular addition to Mac these days. But be careful with the truffle oil. It is too frequently used with a heavy hand, which can be overwhelming. All good things in moderation!

Pumpkin Linguini with Fennel, Ricotta, and Amaretto

MAKES ABOUT 2 SERVINGS

Pumpkin and amaretto have a long history of togetherness in Italy, where both the winter squash and almonds are plentiful. If you can find amoretti cookies, they make the very best topping for this dish. Toasted almonds are second best.

Ingredients

1 medium pumpkin, peeled, seeded, and cut into large chunks

1 bulb fennel

2–4 tablespoons olive oil

2 cloves garlic, minced

½ cup sliced almonds

1 teaspoon fresh marjoram or oregano

1 cup white wine

1 cup ricotta cheese

½ teapsoon kosher salt

½ teaspoon freshly ground black pepper

2 amaretti cookies, crushed

Method

1. Spiralize pumpkin and fennel into thick shreds using the largest holes. Set aside.

2. Heat oil in a large sauté pan over medium heat. Add garlic, almonds, marjoram, and cook until fragrant, about 1 minute. Add fennel and pumpkin. Cook, stirring, until tender, about 5 minutes.

3. Add wine and cook until the liquid is reduced. Add ricotta, salt, pepper, and stir to thoroughly coat. Serve hot with a sprinkling of crushed amaretto cookies.

Spiralized Eggplant Parmesan Bake

MAKES ABOUT 4 SERVINGS

Eggplant Parm is delicious because it is usually really fatty. This baked version emphasizes veggies over fat, but doesn't sacrifice flavor.

Ingredients

3 large Japanese eggplant
2 tablespoons kosher salt
2 tablespoons olive oil,
    extra virgin or regular
1 small red onion, chopped
3 cloves garlic
1 teaspoon dried oregano
1 teaspoon dried basil
½ teaspoon dried thyme
1 cup red wine
1 12-ounce can crushed
    tomatoes
1 tablespoon tomato paste
Kosher salt and freshly
    ground black pepper, to
    taste
8 ounces ricotta cheese
8 ounces fresh buffalo moz-
    zarella, sliced
bread crumbs
½ cup parmesan cheese

Method

1. Spiralize the eggplant using the straight blade to create flat spiral ribbons. Toss them with the salt to coat evenly, place in a colander, and set aside at room temperature. The salt will leach out the moisture, reduce the bitterness, and make the eggplant more flavor absorbent.

2. Heat 1 tablespoon of oil in a large saucepan over medium heat. Add onion and cook, stirring, until it begins to caramelize. Add garlic, dried herbs, and cook another minute. Add wine and cook, stirring, until the liquid is reduced by half. Add tomatoes, tomato paste, and simmer for 20–30 minutes. Remove from heat, season with salt and pepper, and set aside to cool.

3. Preheat oven to 350°F. Rinse the salt off of the eggplant and pat dry.

4. In a large baking dish layer the ingredients in the following order: eggplant, tomato sauce, ricotta, and mozzarella. Repeat this pattern, doing your best to distribute the ingredients evenly across each layer.

5. In a small bowl combine the remaining oil with bread crumbs and parmesan cheese. Mix together to moisten evenly, then distribute evenly across the top as the final layer of the dish.

6. Cover the dish and bake until bubbly, about 30 minutes. Remove cover and cook an additional 5–10 minutes to brown the top and evaporate any excess liquids. Serve hot.

Sweet Potato Pad Thai

MAKES ABOUT 2 SERVINGS

Rice was a major export for Thailand in the 1930s and 40s. In an effort to reduce domestic consumption, Pad Thai, made with rice noodles, was heavily promoted by the government. It's popularity spread after World War II, and it has since become one of that country's national dishes. They could have really saved rice if they had made this spiralized version.

Ingredients

1 block of firm tofu
3 sweet potatoes
Grated zest and juice of
    1 lime
2 tablespoons Thai fish
    sauce
1 tablespoon soy sauce
2 tablespoons Thai chili
    sauce
1 tablespoon honey
2–4 tablespoons coconut or
    peanut oil
3 eggs, cracked and
    whisked together
1 clove garlic, minced
3 green onions, chopped
1 tablespoon freshly grated
    ginger root
1 tablespoon cider vinegar
¼ cup peanuts, shelled and
    chopped
¼ cup cilantro leaves,
    chopped

Method

1. Unwrap the tofu and press it between two plates to remove some of its moisture (as described in the Red Curry recipe on page 76).

2. Spiralize sweet potatoes into thin shreds using the smallest holes. Set aside. In a small bowl stir together lime zest and juice, fish sauce, soy sauce, chili sauce, and honey. Set aside.

3. Heat 1 tablespoon of oil in a large saute pan over medium heat. Add eggs and scramble until set. Remove from the pan and set aside.

4. In the same pan, heat another 1–2 tablespoons oil. Dice tofu into 1-inch cubes and add to the hot oil. Add the garlic, green onions, ginger, and cook, stirring, until translucent. Add vinegar and ½ cup water to deglaze the pan, then add the sweet potato. Sauté until tender and the liquid is evaporated, about 5 minutes.

5. Add the fish sauce mixture to pan, and toss to coat. Add reserved scrambled egg, peanuts, and ¼ cup cilantro. Combine well, divide between serving plates, and serve, garnished with a sprinking of the remaining cilantro.

(continued)

Sweet Potato Pad Thai *(continued)*

VARIATIONS

Protein: This dish is commonly made with shrimp, crab, or chicken. Cook raw meats first with the garlic and ginger. Or fold in precooked meat, warming it through at the end when the vinegar and water is added.

Extra Garnish: Street stalls in Thailand offer myriad garnishing options. Try it with bean sprouts, limes, pickled vegetables, and even banana flowers.

Summer Squash with Tomato Vodka Cream Sauce

MAKES ABOUT 4 SERVINGS

This sauce became all the rage in the Italian restaurants of the late 1990s. Rumor has it that it's not Italian at all, but American. Worse yet, it is said that the recipe was pushed by a vodka company in an effort to sell more hooch. Not that I really care. It's delicious, regardless of its provenance.

Ingredients

2 – 4 tablespoons olive oil

1 red onion

3 cloves garlic

1 teaspoon dried oregano

1 teaspoon dried basil

½ teaspoon dried thyme

¼ teaspoon (a hefty pinch) of red chile flakes, crushed

½ cup vodka

1 12-ounce can crushed tomatoes

1 tablespoon tomato paste

kosher salt and freshly ground black pepper, to taste

2 large zucchini

2 large yellow squash

6 large pattypan squash

1 cup heavy cream

½ cup freshly grated parmesan cheese

Method

1. Heat 2 tablespoons of oil in a large saucepan over medium heat. Add onion and cook, stirring, until they begin to caramelize. Add garlic, dried herbs, chile flakes, and cook another minute. Add vodka, tomatoes and tomato paste, and simmer for 20–30 minutes. Season with salt and pepper, and keep warm.

2. Spiralize zucchini, yellow, and pattypan squashes into thin shreds using the smallest holes. Add them to the sauce, along with the cream, and cook, tossing to coat evenly, until tender. Season with salt and pepper, and serve topped with a sprinkling of parmesan cheese.

Sweet Potato Croque Madam

MAKES 2 SERVINGS

Jumping right on the trendy "ramen burger" bandwagon, this is a creative take on the classic French grilled ham and cheese. (Without the egg it is a croque monsieur). It has a few additional steps, but they are well worth the extra effort. You can easily make the sweet potato "bread" a day ahead, which will speed the final cooking time. And it is the perfect bun for the Curried Cauliflower, Cabbage and White Bean Hamburger Patties *on page 113.*

Ingredients

2 sweet potatoes
3 eggs
½ teaspoon kosher salt
¼ teaspoon freshly ground
   black pepper
1–2 tablespoons olive oil
2–4 tablespoons unsalted
   butter
8–12 slices Ibérico ham
   (or your favorite ham)
8–12 slices gruyère cheese

Method

1. Bring a large saucepan of water to a boil. Spiralize sweet potatoes into thin shreds using the smallest holes. Cook them in the boiling water until tender, about 2–3 minutes. Drain, cool slightly, then combine in a bowl with 1 egg, salt, and pepper. Mix together to evenly coat sweet potato.

2. Heat oil in a large sauté pan over medium heat. Divide potato into four portions, and form each into a patty. Drop carefully into the oil, and fry until golden brown, about 3–5 minutes on each side. Press flat with a spatula when you flip them. Reduce heat, cover, and cook until the center is tender, another 3–5 minutes. Remove from pan, blot off oil on paper towels, and set aside to cool at room temperature.

3. Melt 1 tablespoon of butter in a large nonstick frying pan. Carefully crack in the eggs without breaking the yolks, and fry over easy. Remove the pan from the heat when they are cooked, and set aside.

4. Layer 2 slices of ham between two slices of cheese, and place them on one sweet potato "bun." Slide an egg on top of each, and top with second bun. Place sandwiches in the frying pan over low heat, cover, and cook until cheese melts, about 5 minutes. Serve warm.

VARIATIONS

Potato Options: The same recipe can be made using russet, rose, new, fingerling, or purple potatoes.

Caramelized Onions: Sweet, luscious caramelized onions make a terrific addition to this sandwich. Spiralize a large yellow onion into thin shreds using the smallest holes, and cook in butter, slowly, over medium-low heat until they are dark golden, at least 30 minutes.

Béchamel Sauce: Classic croques contain a smear of this mother sauce. Melt a tablespoon of butter, add a little onion, and cook until translucent. Add a tablespoon of flour, whisk until it is absorbed, then slowly add a cup of milk, whisking. Season with a pinch of freshly grated nutmeg, salt, and pepper. Voilà!

Potato Club

MAKES 2 SERVINGS

This is a fun take on a classic sandwich, and a perfect variation for those trying to avoid bread. You can take it a step further and make it an all-veggie club, although in that case, it's really more of a stacked salad.

Ingredients

1 small purple onion

2 large russet potatoes

2–4 tablespoon olive oil regular

¼ teaspoon kosher salt

1 large, ripe tomato

1 ripe avocado

½ large English or 1 Persian cucumber

1 cup alfalfa sprouts

1 teaspoon red wine vinegar

¼ teaspoon freshly ground black pepper

¼ teaspoon Italian herb blend

4–6 ounces roasted chicken or turkey

4 slices bacon, cooked

6–8 slices Swiss cheese

Method

1. Spiralize onion into thin shreds using the smallest holes. Soak in cold water for at least 10 minutes to remove some of the bitter oils. Spiralize potatoes into thin shreds using the smallest holes, and set aside.

2. Heat oil in a large sauté pan over medium heat. Gather potato into 2–3 inch patties. Place them carefully in the hot pan (do not overcrowd), sprinkle with salt, and fry until golden brown on the bottom, about 3–5 minutes. Flip, press flat with a spatula, reduce heat, cover, and cook until the center is tender, another 5–8 minutes. (Feel free to add a little more oil if necessary after you flip.) Remove from pan, blot off oil on paper towels, and set aside to cool at room temperature. Work in batches with remaining potato.

3. Thinly slice tomato and avocado. Combine in a large bowl with the onions, cucumbers, and alfalfa sprouts. Add 1 tablespoon of olive oil, vinegar, salt, pepper, and herbs, then toss to coat evenly.

4. Layer one potato "bun" with chicken, onion, tomato, bacon, avocado, and sprouts. Top with cheese and the second potato "bun." Skewer with a toothpick to serve.

Vegetarian Club: You could simply omit the offending ingredients, but why not bulk it up with a couple umami-laced elements to counter all that rabbit food? Sauté, broil, or grill large portabella or shitake mushrooms and add them to the mix. And how about a handful of roasted spiralized eggplant? (Use the straight blade to create flat spiral ribbons, salt the eggplant and let it sit for 15 minutes before roasting it in a little oil.) Or try fire-roasted bell peppers. Cook them on the grill, or over a gas burner (right on the flame) until they are well charred. Place in a paper or plastic bag, seal, and let cool. The charred skin will rub right off the cooled peppers, leaving behind its smoky flavor.

sides

Throughout the history of cooking, vegetables have been relegated to supporting roles. While unfair to these talented players, it certainly has provided us a wealth of ideas. Of course, there is nothing to keep you from serving any of these as a main course. The best cooks are always rebellious.

Chayote Squash with Lime and Pumpkin Seeds

MAKES ABOUT 4 SERVINGS

Chayote squash is a mild firm squash used extensively in Latin American cuisines. Its relatively neutral flavor and firm texture make it a perfect backdrop for more complex flavor parings. See the variations below for some more ideas with chayote.

Ingredients

1 cup pumpkin seeds
   (aka pepitas)
3 chayote squash, peeled
3 tablespoons olive oil
1 clove garlic, minced
Grated zest and juice of
   1 lime
½ teaspoon kosher salt
½ cup cilantro leaves,
   chopped

Method

1. Preheat oven to 350°F. Spread the pumpkin seeds out onto a dry baking sheet in a single layer. Bake until toasted and fragrant, about 5 minutes. When you hear the seeds begin to pop, you know they're ready. Set aside to cool at room temperature.

2. Spiralize chayote using the straight blade to create flat spiral ribbons. Set aside.

Heat oil in a large sauté pan over medium heat. Add garlic and cook until just tender, about 30 seconds. Add chayote, and cook just to warm through, about 1–2 minutes. Remove from heat, add lime zest and juice, salt, cilantro, and toasted pumpkin seeds. Toss to coat. Serve warm, or chill and serve as a cold salad.

(continued)

Chayote Squash *(continued)*

Raw: Chayote is just as nice uncooked. Try it raw in this, or any other, salad.

Pico de Gallo: Turn this dish into a fresh salsa with the addition of your ripest tomatoes, spiralized purple onion, cucumber, and jicama. Add a little freshly toasted and ground cumin, and it's a salsa salad!

Curry: Add some plumped golden raisins, and replace the pumpkin seeds with almonds. Add, along with the lime zest, ¼ cup of yogurt or sour cream, and 1 tablespoon of your favorite curry powder or paste.

Garlic Sweet Potato Fries

MAKES ABOUT 2 TO 4 SERVINGS

I like to use the red yam for this recipe, which is actually a sweet potato. Real yams are much too sweet, and often end up burning.

Ingredients

3 large sweet potatoes
2–4 tablespoons olive oil
4 cloves garlic, minced
¼ cup parsley leaves,
    chopped
½ teaspoon kosher salt
ketchup (see page 146 for
    a homemade ketchup
    recipe)

Method

1. Preheat oven to 400°F. Spiralize sweet potatoes into thick shreds using the larger holes.

2. Toss sweet potatoes with 1–2 tablespoon oil and spread on a baking sheet in an even layer. Bake for 20–30 minutes. Toss the potatoes around the sheet pan a bit after 10 minutes to promote even cooking. When they're done the sweet potatoes should be golden brown, crisp on the edges, and tender on the inside.

3. Meanwhile, heat remaining oil in a small saucepan. Add garlic and cook slowly, over low heat, until tender, but not browned. Remove from heat, add half of the salt and all the parsley. Sprinkle cooked sweet potatoes with remaining salt, then toss quickly with garlic oil before serving hot.

Homemade Ketchup

MAKES ABOUT 1 QUART OF KETCHUP

This is fun, primarily because it's something no one expects anymore. Also, it's easy. Easy + Fun = Delicious.

Ingredients

1 tablespoon olive oil

1 yellow onion

2 cloves garlic

2 stalks celery

1 inch fresh ginger root

½ teaspoon crushed whole allspice

1 cinnamon stick, crushed

2–3 whole cloves

½ teaspoon cayenne pepper

1 teaspoon dry mustard

½ cup cider or white wine vinegar

⅓ cup brown sugar

1 28-ounce can crushed tomatoes

1 tablespoon tomato paste

½ teaspoon kosher salt

½ teaspoon white pepper

Method

1. Heat oil in a large saucepan over high heat. Add onion, garlic, celery, ginger root, and cook, stirring, until the onions begin to brown slightly. Add allspice, cinnamon, cloves, cayenne, mustard, vinegar, and sugar. Reduce heat to a simmer and cook 10 minutes, stirring occasionally.

2. Add tomatoes and tomato paste, and simmer for 20–30 minutes, stirring occasionally. Remove from heat, and cool to room temperature.

3. Transfer to a blender or food processor and puree until very smooth. Test consistency. If the mixture seems thin, return it to the stove and cook on a low simmer for 10–15 minutes to thicken.

4. Season with salt and pepper, and cool completely. Store refrigerated in airtight containers for several weeks, or freeze for longer storage. This recipe can also be processed in canning jars. Consult the instructions that accompany the jars.

Homemade Mayonnaise

MAKES ABOUT 1 TO 1½ CUPS

My family thinks I'm weird, but I love my fries with mayo. Not to be snobby, but I learned it in France. Millions of Frenchies can't all be wrong. I prefer to make my own mayo, which is, I admit, super snobby. C'est la vie.

Ingredients

1 egg yolk
½ teaspoon Dijon mustard
¼ teaspoon kosher salt
1 cup vegetable oil
1 tablespoon lemon juice
Pinch of white pepper

Method

1. In a large bowl combine yolk, mustard, and salt, and whisk together. Slowly, drop by drop, add ¾ cups of the oil, whisking vigorously all the time. This emulsifies the mixture.

2. Stir in the lemon juice, then resume adding the remaining oil, whisking the whole time. When all the oil is in, season with white pepper, and more salt if necessary. Store refrigerated in airtight containers for several weeks.

VARIATIONS

Oils: Some interesting mayo can be made by using different oils. Olive oil is nice, as are some more interesting nut or seed oils. Feel free to experiment! It is advisable to still use at least ½ cup of vegetable oil, as most specialty oils have pretty strong flavors.

Aioli: Add 1–2 heads of roasted garlic to the yolk, and continue as directed. To roast garlic, brush a whole head with oil, wrap in foil, and bake for 30–40 minutes, until soft. Cool and squeeze!

Curly Oven Fries

MAKES ABOUT 2 TO 4 SERVINGS

These are so popular it would be a shame to not include them in this book. See the variations below for a variety of spice mixtures, and different vegetables to "fry."

Ingredients

3 large russet potatoes
2–3 tablespoons olive oil regular
½ teaspoon kosher salt
ketchup (see page 146 for a homemade ketchup recipe)

Method

1. Preheat oven to 400°F. Spiralize potatoes into thick shreds using the larger holes.

2. Toss potatoes with oil and spread on a baking sheet in an even layer. Bake for 20–30 minutes. Toss the potatoes around the sheet pan a bit after 10 minutes to promote even cooking. When they're done the potatoes should be golden brown, crisp on the edges, and tender on the inside. Sprinkle with salt before serving hot.

VARIATIONS

Fat-Free: If you are watching fat intake, try this method. It takes a little more attention than the recipe above, but is no less satisfying. Instead of oil, toss the potatoes in one egg white. Get them well coated, then bake as directed with additional stirring every 5 minutes to promote even crisping.

Spicy Fries: Before they go into the oven, sprinkle your potatoes with your favorite Cajun, ranch, or curry seasoning.

Fancy Salt: This is the perfect vehicle for that fancy salt you bought but don't know what to do with.

Potato Options: This recipe works perfectly with a variety of potatoes.

Yellow Squash with Edamame and Sesame

MAKES ABOUT 4 SERVINGS

Black sesame seeds are just like the white ones, except, of course, they're black. And as with the white ones, toasting brings out their flavor. But be very careful when toasting black sesame seeds. You can't really see when the toasting is complete. Let your nose be the judge, and pull them off the heat when they start to smell good.

Ingredients

3 large yellow squash
¼ cup black sesame seeds
1 tablespoon sesame oil
1 clove garlic, minced
3 green onions, chopped
1 tablespoon freshly grated
   ginger root
1 tablespoon rice vinegar
2 tablespoons soy sauce
1½ cups edamame beans,
   removed from their pods,
   blanched and salted
½ cup cilantro leaves
1 cup chive buds or 1-inch
   lengths of fresh chives

Method

1. Spiralize yellow squash into thin shreds using the smallest holes. Set aside. In a small sauté pan toast sesame seeds over high heat for 1 minute, or until fragrant. Pour them off the hot pan as soon as they are done, and set aside.

2. Heat sesame oil in a large sauté pan over medium heat. Add garlic, green onions, ginger, and cook for 1 minute, until translucent. Deglaze with vinegar and soy sauce. Add squash and cook until tender, about 1–2 minutes. Add edamame, cilantro, chive buds, toasted sesame seeds, and cook, tossing to distribute ingredients and to warm through. Serve warm, or chill and use as a cold salad.

VARIATION

Tropical Twist: This combination is delightful with a little exotic sweetness. Add to the deglaze 1 cup of coconut milk. Add with the edamame 1 cup of chopped fresh pineapple. Then finish it all off with the grated zest and juice of 1 lime.

Purple Potatoes with Quinoa, Berries, and Almonds

MAKES ABOUT 4 SERVINGS

Purple potatoes are some of the oldest potato species known to man. Native to the high plains and mountain slopes of the Andes, they have been cultivated for 8,000 years. There are several purple varieties that include many different shapes and sizes. For spiralizing, the larger the better.

Ingredients

1½ cups quinoa
¼ teaspoon kosher salt
1 cup sliced almonds
4 large purple Peruvian potatoes
2–4 tablespoons olive oil
1 tablespoon balsamic vinegar
1 clove garlic, minced
1 pint blueberries
¼ cup fresh mint leaves, chopped
Kosher salt and freshly ground black pepper, to taste

Method

1. Preheat oven to 375°F. Combine quinoa, 2 cups of water, and salt in a medium saucepan and bring to a boil over high heat. At the boil, reduce to low and simmer, covered, for 15 minutes. Remove from heat and set aside at room temperature to absorb all liquid.

2. Spread almonds out onto a dry baking sheet and bake until toasted and fragrant, about 5 minutes. Set aside to cool at room temperature.

3. Spiralize potatoes using the straight blade to create flat spiral ribbons. Toss in 1–2 tablespoons of oil, then spread out the ribbons onto a baking sheet. Bake until tender and golden around the edges, about 10–15 minutes.

4. In a large bowl stir together remaining tablespoon of oil with vinegar, garlic, berries, and mint. Add quinoa, almonds, and potatoes, and toss together to coat evenly. Serve warm, or refrigerate and serve chilled. Season with salt and pepper.

Grain Options: Why not try something more exotic? Try some of the more unusual grains now on the market, like Kamut or spelt. Or use widely available brown rice or barley. You really can't go wrong with any grain.

Grain Free: Avoiding grains altogether? Substitute some beans for the quinoa. Try garbanzo or black beans for a protein-rich version.

Berry Options: Any berry will work, but if it's not berry season, consider adding dried fruit. Dried blueberries are available in some stores, or use dried cranberries, cherries, figs, or good ole raisins.

Onion Strings

MAKES ABOUT 4 SERVINGS

Be sure your onions are at room temperature for this recipe. If you chill them, their sugar content increases, and they will burn faster in the high heat of the oil.

Ingredients

1 cup all-purpose flour
   (whole wheat or gluten-
   free flours work, too)
½ teaspoon kosher salt,
   plus extra to finish
½ teaspoon freshly ground
   black pepper
1 large yellow onion
1 large white onion
1 large red onion
1 cup vegetable oil

Method

1. In a large bowl combine the flour, salt, and pepper. Spiralize onions into thin shreds using the smallest holes, then add to the flour and toss to evenly coat. Let the onions sit in the flour for 5–10 minutes. This allows the onion's moisture to absorb the flour, making the finished product crisper.

2. Heat oil in a large skillet over high heat. Place onions in oil carefully (do not crowd them) and fry until golden brown, about 3–5 minutes. Drain on paper towels and sprinkle with salt. Repeat with remaining onions. Serve immediately.

VARIATIONS

Fancy Finish: Instead of plain salt at the end, sprinkle on a mixture of fresh herbs minced with salt. Or try a Cajun seasoning, or a single fancy salt.

Onion or Shallots: This recipe can easily be made with only one variety of onion, as well as spiralized shallots.

154   The Spiralized Kitchen

Sautéed Purple Cabbage with Bacon and Caraway

MAKES ABOUT 4 SERVINGS

This is one of my favorite sides, because I love the flavor of caraway. But not everyone shares my affection. If you are not a caraway lover, try replacing it with celery seed, dill seeds, or dried dill weed.

Ingredients

1 head purple cabbage

6 slices bacon, preferably thick-cut

2 tablespoons caraway seeds

1 yellow onion, sliced

2 cloves garlic, minced

¼ cup white wine vinegar

2 tablespoons honey

½ teaspoon kosher salt

½ teaspoon freshly ground black pepper

1 cup pecan pieces, toasted

Method

1. Spiralize cabbage using the straight blade to create flat ribbons. Set aside.

2. Cook bacon in a large sauté pan over medium heat. When the fat has rendered out, and meat is crisp, remove the meat and set aside. Drain off all but 2 tablespoons of bacon fat. Add caraway seeds, onion, and cook until translucent. Add garlic, vinegar, and honey, and stir to combine.

3. Add cabbage and cook, tossing to evenly coat and distribute ingredients. When cabbage is wilted and softened season with salt and pepper. Toss in toasted pecans and crumbled cooked bacon just before serving.

Roasted Beets with Horseradish

MAKES ABOUT 4 SERVINGS

Bright fuchsia red beets are amazing, and one of my favorite ingredients. But beets are readily available in other colors, too. Try this recipe with an array of colorful beets when they become available in the late summer. For the rest of the year, red will do.

Ingredients

2 large red beets

2 large golden beets

2 tablespoons olive oil, extra virgin or regular

3 green onions, chopped

2 tablespoons freshly grated horseradish root, or 1 tablespoon prepared horseradish.

Grated zest and juice of 1 lemon

½ teaspoon kosher salt

Method

1. Preheat oven to 375°F. Spiralize beets using the straight blade to create flat spiral ribbons. Combine in a large bowl with 1 tablespoon olive oil. Toss to coat, spread out onto a baking sheet, and roast until tender and browned on the edges, about 10–15 minutes.

2. Toss roasted beets with remaining oil, green onions, horseradish, lemon zest and juice, and salt before serving.

VARIATION

Nut It Up: This dish would be delightful with a crunchy element. Try it with toasted pistachios or cashews. (Gesundheit!)

Rutabaga White Bean Gratin

MAKES ABOUT 4 SERVINGS

Au Gratin is the French term that refers to browning the top of a dish, usually covered with cheese, bread crumbs, or an egg-based custard. This is typically baked in a shallow ceramic dish, which cooks faster, but you should use whatever you've got.

Ingredients

4–5 large rutabagas
2 tablespoons olive oil
1 yellow onion, sliced
2 cloves garlic, minced
1 tablespoon fresh thyme
  leaves, chopped
1 8-ounce can white beans,
  drained
½ teaspoon kosher salt
¼ teaspoon white pepper
1 cup ricotta cheese
¼ cup freshly grated par-
  mesan cheese

Method

1. Preheat oven to 350°F. Bring a large pot of water to a boil over high heat. Spiralize the rutabaga using the straight blade to create flat spiral ribbons. Add to the boiling water and cook until tender, about 1–2 minutes. Drain and set aside.

2. Heat oil in a large sauté pan over medium heat. Add onion and cook until translucent, about 2–3 minutes. Add garlic and thyme, and cook until garlic just begins to color. Remove from heat and add white beans, salt, and pepper. Stir thoroughly to combine.

3. Assemble the gratin by layering rutabaga, bean mixture, and ricotta cheese in a shallow baking dish. Repeat until all ingredients are in. Top with parmesan cheese, cover, and bake until bubbly and tender, about 15–20 minutes. Uncover and cook another 10 minutes to brown the top. Serve hot.

Goat Cheese: For a tangier version, replace the ricotta with a soft chevre.

Caramelized Onion: Enhance the sweetness of this dish by doubling the onion, and cooking them very slowly, over low heat, until they are a rich, dark, golden brown. Then proceed with the recipe as written.

Roasted Root Vegetables with Cider Glaze

MAKES ABOUT 4 SERVINGS

This classic autumnal recipe is easy and good all year long. Don't save it for fall! It's a great accompaniment to grilled summer meats!

Ingredients

1 butternut squash

1 sweet potato

1 red beet

1 parsnip

1 yellow onion, sliced

1–2 tablespoons olive oil

1 teaspoon kosher salt

1 tablespoon unsalted
   butter

2 cloves garlic

1 tablespoon honey

1 tablespoon cider vinegar

1 cup apple juice

½ cup toasted pecans,
   chopped

Method

1. Preheat oven to 375°F. Spiralize squash, potato, beet, parsnip, and onion into thick shreds using the largest holes. Toss in olive oil, and spread onto a baking sheet. Roast until tender and crisp on the outside. Sprinkle with salt and keep warm.

2. Meanwhile heat butter in a large sauté pan over medium heat. Add garlic and cook until translucent, about 30–60 seconds. Stir in honey, vinegar, and apple juice. Bring to a boil and cook, stirring, until reduced to a syrup consistency, about 3–5 minutes. Keep your eye on this. It will happen fast!

3. Pour the glaze over warm roasted roots, toss to coat, and serve hot, topped with toasted pecans.

VARIATIONS

Bacon: Use two slices of raw diced bacon instead of butter here. Render the fat and crisp it up in the pan, then add the garlic, etc.

Cheesy: Garnish this dish with a crumble of feta, goat, or sharp blue cheese. The salty tang is a great contrast to the sweetness of these roots and the apple juice.

Spiralized Chinese Fried "Rice"

MAKES ABOUT 4 SERVINGS

This is strictly vegetable rice, for those of you avoiding carbs. It would be great, however, with added grain, too. See the variations for some ideas.

Ingredients

1 large carrot

1 large sweet potato

1 large rutabaga

1 large zucchini

1–2 tablespoons peanut or vegetable oil

2 eggs

2 teaspoons sesame oil

3 green onions, chopped

2 cloves garlic, minced

2 tablespoons freshly grated ginger

1 tablespoon honey

2 tablespoons soy sauce

1 tablespoon rice vinegar

2 tablespoons peas, fresh or frozen

½ cup fresh cilantro leaves

Method

1. Spiralize carrot, sweet potato, and rutabaga into thin shreds using the smallest holes. Break by hand or chop them into about ½-inch lengths. Set aside. Spiralize the zucchini into the same size, and set it aside separately.

2. Heat vegetable oil in a large wok, sauté pan, or griddle. Whisk the eggs together, then add them to the hot oil, scrambling, until solidified, about 30–60 seconds. Remove from pan, set aside, and return pan to the heat.

3. Add sesame oil to the pan, then add green onions, garlic, ginger, and cook to soften, less than a minute. Add spiralized carrot, sweet potato, and rutabaga. Cook, stirring, until the roots begin to brown. Add honey, soy, and vinegar. Add peas and zucchini, and cook until warmed through. Remove from heat, and fold in egg, cilantro, and serve.

VARIATIONS

Meaty Rice: Feel free to add the traditional pork, chicken, or shrimp into this dish. If you're using raw meat, add it to the oil first, before the roots go in. If you have precooked meat, add it with the zucchini.

Grainy : You can easily add rice to this dish. It must be precooked, and be added with the roots. This is a great vehicle for using up any leftover grain you might have.

Spiralized Latkes

MAKES ?

There are as many recipes for latkes as there are potato lovers. This one is my favorite. If you are avoiding gluten, see the flour-free variation below.

Ingredients

2 large russet potatoes

1 yellow onion

2 eggs

2 tablespoons all purpose flour (whole wheat and gluten-free flours work, too)

½ teaspoon kosher salt

½ teaspoon freshly ground black pepper

4–8 tablespoons vegetable oil

4–8 tablespoons butter

Apple sauce

Sour cream

Method

1. Spiralize potatoes and onion into thin shreds using the smallest holes. Combine them in a large bowl with eggs, flour, salt and pepper, and toss them together well.

2. Heat 2 tablespoons of oil and butter in a large sauté pan over high heat. Gather up the potato into walnut-sized bundles and place them in the hot oil. (Be careful, the oil might splatter.) Press them into flat discs, and cook on high heat for 1–2 minutes. Shake the pan occasionally to keep them from sticking. Reduce the heat and cook until the bottom is golden brown and set. Flip and repeat on the other side. Add another dollop of butter or oil as necessary for even browning. When golden on both sides, transfer from the sauté pan to a paper towel–lined baking sheet and sprinkle with salt. Keep these warm in the oven, while you repeat with the remaining potato. Serve with optional toppings of apple sauce and sour cream.

Potato Options: These can be made with any potato, but the sweeter and waxier ones need to be watched carefully to avoid burning. You can also try it with another root vegetable, such as carrots or rutabagas. Get creative!

Flour-Free: It's as easy as just leaving the flour out of this recipe. You can, in fact, make these with no egg either, and many people do. (I'm talking to you, vegans!) There is enough starch in a freshly grated potato to hold it together well. The method is less successful with sweet potato and other roots that naturally contain less starch.

baking & desserts

The spiralizer is in no way limited to the savory side of the kitchen. Get your sweet on with the following spiralicious treats.

Apple-Cinnamon Fritters

MAKES ABOUT 6 SERVINGS

These easy treats are suitable for breakfast, dessert, or a well-deserved mid-afternoon snack. Even if you don't really deserve it, you should try them.

Ingredients

2 cups all-purpose flour
  (whole wheat and gluten-
  free flours work, too)
2¼ teaspoons baking
  powder
½ cup brown sugar
1¼ teaspoons kosher salt
½ teaspoon cinnamon
2 large eggs
¾ cup milk
1 teaspoon vanilla extract
3 large Fuji apples
¼–½ cup vegetable or
  peanut oil

Method

1. In a large bowl sift together flour, baking powder, sugar, salt, and cinnamon. In a separate bowl, whisk together egg, milk, and vanilla. Add the liquid to the dry ingredients, and stir together quickly with as few strokes as possible.

2. Spiralize apples into thin shreds using the smallest holes. Add them to the batter, stir to coat, then set aside to rest at room temperature for 10 minutes. This rest time gives the baking powder a chance to react to the moisture, which will make the fritters lighter and fluffier.

3. Heat 2–3 inches of oil in a large saucepan over high heat until it reaches 375°F. You can use a deep-fry thermometer, or just wait until a small bit of food tossed in begins bubbling immediately. At that point, reduce the heat to medium. Continue to monitor the temperature in the same way. If the batter browns too fast, turn down the heat. If it takes too long to brown, turn it up.

4. Gather ¼-cup-sized bundles of battered apples and drop them carefully in the oil. Do not overcrowd. Cook until golden brown on each side, about 1–2 minutes per side. Remove with a slotted spoon and drain on paper towels. Repeat with remaining batter. Serve hot, dusted with powdered sugar.

(continued)

Apple Cinnamon Fritters *(continued)*

Fruit Options: This will work great with pears, persimmons, and even berries. Add a pint of blueberries into this batter, along with the apples, or forget the apples altogether and use 3 pints of mixed berries. They look a little lumpier than the apple version, but are no less delicious.

Pumpkin: Spiralize a pumpkin or butternut squash in the same manner, then cook briefly in boiling water to tenderize. Drain well, pat dry, then add to the batter. For a more pumpkiny taste, add ½ teaspoon nutmeg and ¼ teaspoon clove with the cinnamon.

Asian Pear Dessert Salad

MAKES ABOUT 4 SERVINGS

Having a salad for dessert sounds weird, I know—until you taste this recipe! Do not confuse it with Ambrosia, Seafoam Salad, or other Jell-O based lunch counter favorites from days gone by. This is a fresh blend of ripe, raw fruits, and is a perfect finish to a rich meal.

Ingredients

1 tablespoon sugar

1 teaspoon orange flower water

Grated zest and juice of 1 orange

Pinch kosher salt

3 Asian Pears

½ cup pomegranate seeds (or 1 cup fresh berries)

¼ cup of fresh mint leaves, minced

3–4 gingersnap cookies, crumbled

Method

1. In a small saucepan bring 1 tablespoon of water and sugar to a boil over high heat. At the boil, remove from heat. (This is simple syrup.) Add orange flower water, orange zest and juice, salt, and set aside to cool.

2. Spiralize the Asian pear using the straight blade to create flat spiral ribbons. Combine them in a large bowl with pomegranate seeds and mint. Toss with dressing, and serve, chilled or at room temperature, sprinkled with gingersnap crumbs.

VARIATIONS

Accompaniments: This salad is also great topped with a dollop of whipped cream, vanilla yogurt, ice cream, or sorbet. It also benefits from a salty crumbled cheese, like blue or feta.

Sugar-Free: If you are trying to avoid processed sugar, use agave syrup, honey, or a sugar substitute in the syrup. Or you can omit it altogether and rely on the natural fruit's sweetness, which is ample. Then, replace the cookies with chopped nuts for a little crunch. Try almonds or brazil nuts.

Sautéed Pears with Brown Sugar and Rum

MAKES ABOUT 4 SERVINGS

My favorite dessert of all time is a cheese and fruit plate. Slightly sweetened, these pears become a perfect counterpoint to saltier cheeses. Here we serve figs, with Manchego cheese and candied walnuts. This would be just as delicious accompanied by a scoop of Pecan Praline ice cream.

Ingredients

- 3 Bosc pears (Bosc pears are used here because they are firm when ripe, and keep their shape when cooked.)
- 2 tablespoons unsalted butter
- 2 tablespoons granulated sugar
- 2 tablespoons brown sugar
- ½ teaspoon kosher salt
- ½ cup apple juice
- ½ cup dark rum (preferably Myers)

Method

1. Remove the seeds from the bottom of the pears using a melon baller. Spiralize them using the straight blade to create flat spiral ribbons. Set aside. (I prefer to keep the skin on my pears for visual effect, but they can certainly be peeled if that's what you prefer.)

2. Melt butter in a large sauté pan over medium heat. Add sugars, salt, and then pears. Sauté 2–3 minutes, stirring, until the sugar liquefies and the pears begin to caramelize. Add the apple juice and cook until the liquid is reduced by half. Add the rum and carefully ignite. Cook until the liquid is reduced by half again, then remove from the heat. Serve warm or at room temperature.

VARIATIONS

Accompaniments: Try this with a scoop of vanilla ice cream, and a sprinkling of toasted pecans.

Fruit Options: This dish works equally well with apples, quince, and persimmons (use the firm fuyu variety for best spiralizing results).

Carrot Cupcakes

MAKES ABOUT A DOZEN CUPCAKES

There are many schools of carrot cake thought. This recipe leans to the simpler variety, because that is what I like, and in these pages I get to pick. But you may easily chunk it up with the addition of dried fruits, pineapple, and nuts. This batter can also be used to make standard cake circles, or a loaf of bread, which is great toasted and smeared with marmalade. See the variations below.

Ingredients

4 large carrots

2 cups granulated sugar

1½ cups vegetable oil

4 eggs

2 cups whole wheat or all-purpose flour (gluten-free flour works, too)

2 teaspoons baking powder

1½ teaspoons baking soda

1 teaspoon kosher salt

1 teaspoon cinnamon

2 teaspoons ground nutmeg

1 teaspoon cardamom

Method

1. Preheat oven to 375°F. Coat muffin tins with pan spray and line with paper muffin cups. Spiralize the carrots into thin shreds using the smallest holes.

2. In a large bowl whisk together sugar, oil, and eggs. Sift and add the flour, baking powder, baking soda, salt, and spices. Stir in carrots.

3. Gather up small portions of carrot from the batter, divide evenly between prepared muffin tins, then fill each cup to the rim with batter. Bake for 15–20 minutes, until the cake springs back to the touch and a pick inserted comes out clean. Remove from the oven, cool 10 minutes, then remove from pan. (This prevents sweating on the bottom, which makes the cakes soggy.) Eat as is, or allow the cupcakes to cool before icing. (See Cream Cheese Frosting recipe on page 174)

Note: Shape Options

This batter can be baked in any pan by simply adjusting the baking time. Larger cakes benefit from a reduced temperature (325–350°F) after 15–20 minutes, to prevent the surface from burning before the center is cooked. Be sure whatever pan you use is sprayed and papered to ensure easy removal.

Cream Cheese Frosting

MAKES ABOUT 4 CUPS

If you finish a carrot cake with anything but this frosting, you'll probably have a revolt on your hands.

Ingredients

2 ounces (½ stick) unsalted
  butter, softened
1 8-ounce package cream
  cheese
1 tablespoon vanilla extract
¼ teaspoon kosher salt
2 teaspoons lemon juice
1 pound powdered sugar,
  sifted

Method

1. Beat butter and cream cheese together to create a smooth paste. Be sure there are no lumps remaining. Stir in vanilla, salt, and lemon juice. Add sifted powdered sugar slowly (to prevent a powdery mess), and stir until smooth. Use immediately, or refrigerated for storage. The frosting must be softened to be used, either by bringing to room temperature or by beating.

Candied Carrot Strings

MAKES ENOUGH CANDIED STRINGS FOR THE ABOVE BATCH OF CUPCAKES

I use this same method for candying citrus zest, ginger, and pineapple.

Ingredients

2 large carrots
1 cup granulated sugar

Method

1. Bring 3 cups of water to boil in a small saucepan. Spiralize the carrots into thin shreds using the smallest holes. Add them to the boiling water and cook for 1 minute to soften. Strain and discard the water.

2. Combine sugar with 1 cup water. Bring to a boil, add carrot, turn down heat and simmer for 10 minutes. Drain off the syrup and spread the carrot strings out onto parchment paper to cool. Toss cooled carrot strings in granulated sugar. Store airtight at room temperature, or in the freezer for extended periods.

Coconut and Carrot Rice Pudding

MAKES ABOUT 6 SERVINGS

Rice pudding is a classic "use up the old stuff" recipe. This version is reminiscent of carrot cake, but is even easier, especially if you are using leftover rice. I like to use brown, arborio, jasmine, or sushi rice here, but anything works.

Ingredients

½ cup golden raisins

¼ cup dark raisins

¼ cup currants

¼ cup chopped pitted dates

2 tablespoons dark rum or brandy

3 large carrots

2 eggs

¼ cup granulated sugar

½ teaspoon ground nutmeg

¼ teaspoon ground cardamom

¼ teaspoon cinnamon

⅛ teaspoon ground clove

1 tablespoon vanilla extract

3 cups heavy cream, half and half, or milk (The cream version will be a little richer, but even non-fat milk works well here. Even water works—but let's not get crazy!)

2 cups cooked rice

1 cup shredded coconut

Method

1. Combine dried fruits, rum, and 1½ cups boiling water. Set aside to plump for at least 30 minutes. Overnight is better.

2. Preheat oven to 375°F. Coat a 9 x13-inch baking dish with pan spray. Spiralize the carrots into thin shreds using the smallest holes. Set aside.

3. Whisk together eggs, sugar, spices, and vanilla. Add cream and mix thoroughly. Stir in rice, carrots, coconut, and drained dried fruits. Transfer the mixture into the prepared baking dish. Bake until the custard has set and the dish is golden brown on the top, about 30–45 minutes. Serve warm or at room temperature with a dollop of whipped cream and a sprinkle of cinnamon sugar.

> **VARIATION**
>
> **Tropical Additions:** Consider giving this dish a tropical twist with chopped mango, pineapple, or banana. You can even add the reconstituted dried versions of those fruits instead of the raisins. And try substituting canned coconut milk for part or all of the cream.

Melon with Spiced Honey Compote

MAKES ABOUT 4 SERVINGS

Melon is a refreshing treat on a hot summer day. This recipe pairs the sweetness of melon with the acidity of honey and the spice of pepper. Try it as is, or spooned over cold, fruity sorbet, ice creams, or Greek yogurt.

Ingredients

3 tablespoons honey

Grated zest and juice of
   1 orange

1 inch of fresh ginger root,
   peeled and grated

1 large honeydew or canta-
   loupe melon

½ teaspoon freshly ground
   black pepper

½ teaspoon freshly ground
   pink peppercorns

5–6 leaves of fresh mint,
   minced

Method

1. In a small saucepan, combine honey, orange zest and juice, and ginger. Bring to a simmer over medium heat, then remove from heat and set aside to cool and steep. (You can also do this step in a microwave.)

2. Using a chef knife, cut the bottom and top off the melon so that it won't roll, then cut off the skin all the way around. Working your way around the fruit from the outside in, shred the melon into long thin strips using the handheld julienne peeler. A standard potato peeler is the next best tool, which will make beautiful long flat ribbons.

3. In a large bowl combine the melon with the honey mixture. Add peppercorns and mint, and toss to coat. The melon loses its vibrant color the longer it sits in the syrup, so add it at the last minute. Serve immediately in chilled glasses as is, or over frozen sorbet, ice cream, or yogurt.

VARIATIONS

Meaty Appetizers: Melon and prosciutto is a classic Italian starter. Consider this variation—the above recipe with the addition of julienne prosciutto—served in chilled cocktail glasses.

Oat Apple Crisp

MAKES ABOUT 4 SERVINGS

A baked fruit crisp is possibly the easiest baked dessert of all time, which is one reason it is so satisfying. The spiralizer gives this old-home, spur-of-the-moment classic a sophisticated look ... kinda like a farm boy in a tuxedo.

Ingredients

5 Fuji apples (or your favorite snackin' apple)

Grated zest and juice of 1 lemon

2 tablespoons all-purpose flour (whole wheat and gluten-free will work, too)

1 tablespoon granulated sugar

½ teaspoon kosher salt

½ teaspoon cinnamon

1 teaspoon freshly grated nutmeg

½ teaspoon ground cardamom

⅛ teaspoon (a tiny pinch) of ground clove

4 ounces (1 stick) plus 2 tablespoons unsalted butter

1 cup whole wheat flour (gluten-free flour works, too)

½ cup brown sugar

½ cup rolled oats

Method

1. Preheat oven to 350°F. Coat a 9 x 13-inch baking dish (or 4 individual baking dishes) with pan spray. Spiralize apples using the straight blade to create flat spiral ribbons. (I like to leave on the skin, but feel free to peel the apples if you prefer.) Toss apples together with lemon zest and juice, flour, granulated sugar, salt, and spices. Arrange these in a baking dish and dot with 2 tablespoons of butter.

2. In a medium bowl combine whole wheat flour, brown sugar, oats, and remaining butter. Cut together until the mixture resembles a coarse crumb mixture. (I like to use my fingertips for this, but a fork or pastry cutter work great, too.) Sprinkle this evenly over the prepared apples in the baking dish.

3. Bake until the filling is bubbly and the crumb topping is golden brown. Serve warm with a scoop of vanilla ice cream or whipped cream.

> **VARIATION**
>
> **Fruity Options:** This recipe works well with pear, quince, persimmon, or firm stone fruits like peaches, nectarines, or plums. Or make it with a mixture. And consider adding berries, figs, or rhubarb to your spiralized fruits.

Peach Melba

This dish is a fresh version of the Escoffier classic. Although it was originally served with raspberry sauce rather than fresh berries, I like nothing better than a whole ripe berry at the peak of its season. If, however, you find yourself making this at any other time of year, see the variation below for raspberry sauce.

Ingredients

3 firm peaches or
    nectarines
1 tablespoon granulated
    sugar
½ teaspoon vanilla extract
1 pint vanilla ice cream
1 pint fresh ripe raspberries

Method

1. Cut peaches in half at its equator, remove the pit, and spiralize using the straight blade to create flat spiral ribbons. Combine them in a bowl with sugar and vanilla. Toss to coat, and set aside to macerate for 5 minutes.

2. Divide macerated peaches between four serving dishes. Top each with a scoop of vanilla ice cream and a handful of raspberries. Serve immediately.

VARIATION

Raspberry Sauce: Combine raspberries in a blender with 1 tablespoon of sugar and 1 tablespoon lemon juice. Blend to a puree, then pass through a fine mesh strainer to remove the seeds.

Pumpkin Cheesecake

MAKES 6 TO 8 SERVINGS

This is a fun version of a holiday favorite. I made them in individual-sized cheesecake rings to show off the spiralized pumpkin, but you can easily bake it in a standard springform pan.

Ingredients

4 ounces graham crackers

1 tablespoon granulated sugar

2 tablespoons unsalted butter, melted

½ small pumpkin or 1 large butternut squash

8 ounces cream cheese, softened

1 cup sugar

Grated zest of 1 orange

¼ teaspoon cinnamon

¼ teaspoon nutmeg

⅛ teaspoon ground clove

¼ teaspoon kosher salt

2 eggs

1 cup sour cream

Method

1. Preheat oven to 350°F. Coat 6 individual cheesecake rings (set on a parchment-lined baking sheet), or one 8-inch springform pan, with pan spray.

2. Combine graham crackers and sugar in a food processor and pulverize to a powder. Add melted butter and pulse to combine. Transfer to prepared pan(s) and press into the bottom, creating a crust approximately ½-inch thick. Bake for 5 minutes to slightly toast and set the crust.

3. Bring a large pot of water to a boil. Peel and seed the pumpkin, cut into large chunks, and spiralize it into thin shreds using the smallest holes. Par-cook in water for 2–3 minutes, until just softened. Drain completely.

4. In a large bowl cream together the cheese and sugar, until smooth and lump free. (Lump free is important!) Stir in orange zest, spices, and salt. Add the eggs one at a time, whisking each until smooth before adding the next.

5. Arrange the well-drained pumpkin on top of the toasted crust, and pour cheesecake mix on top, filling to the rim. Bake for 15–25 minutes (40–50 minutes for large springform), until the cheesecake has slightly souffléed and starts to brown. Cool completely, then chill in the refrigerator for at least 2 hours. The cakes will sink a bit as they chill.

6. Top the cakes with an even layer of sour cream before removing them from the pan. Serve with a sprinkle of toasted pumpkin seeds, rum-soaked raisins, or caramel sauce.

Sweet Potato Pie

MAKE ABOUT 6 TO 8 SERVINGS

This variation of a classic works equally well with butternut squash, pumpkin, or even firm fruits like apples. The key is excess—pile that filling high. The spiralizer creates a lot of air, and the sweet potato will settle as it cooks. You don't want your pie to appear stingy.

Ingredients

3 cups plus 1 tablespoon whole wheat or all-purpose flour (gluten-free flour works here, too)

1 teaspoon kosher salt

1 tablespoon granulated sugar

8 ounces unsalted butter, chilled, plus 2 tablespoons

¼–½ cup ice water

1 teaspoon cider vinegar

4 large sweet potatoes

2 tablespoons brown sugar

1 teaspoon nutmeg

½ teaspoon cinnamon

¼ teaspoon kosher salt

1 egg

Method

1. Combine 3 cups of flour, salt, and sugar in a large bowl. Cut in 8 ounces of butter until the mixture resembles a coarse meal. Using a fork, add water slowly, stirring until a dough is formed. Wrap dough and chill for at least 1 hour (longer is better).

2. Bring a large pot of water to a boil. Spiralize sweet potatoes into thin shreds using the smallest holes. Par-cook in water for 2–3 minutes, until just softened. Drain completely. Combine well-drained sweet potatoes in a large bowl with brown sugar, remaining tablespoon of flour, spices, and salt. Toss to coat thoroughly, and set aside.

3. Coat an 8–9 inch pie pan (or 8 individual pie tins) with pan spray. Using ⅓ of the pie dough, knead it briefly into a round disc, then roll out into a circle ¼-inch thick. Line the bottom of the pan, fill it with the sweet potato mixture, and dot the top with remaining butter. Roll out another circle of dough and use it as the top crust. (You can use it as a solid circle, or cut it into strips and weave it into a lattice.) Crimp the edges, then freeze the pie for about 30 minutes. (This helps maintain the shape of the dough in the oven.) Preheat the oven to 350°F.

(continued)

Sweet Potato Pie *(continued)*

4. Whisk together the egg with 1 tablespoon of water, brush it across the top of the pie, and sprinkle the surface with sugar. (This promotes a golden brown crust.) Bake for 20–30 minutes, until the crust is golden brown. Reduce the oven temperature to 325°F and continue cooking until the filling is bubbly, about another 20 minutes. Cover with foil if the crust starts to get too dark. Remove from oven, cool to room temperature, and serve with whipped cream, vanilla ice cream, or marshmallow fluff.

VARIATIONS

Crumb-Topped Pie: For a different take on top crust, use the streusel topping from the Oat Apple Crisp on page 180. Bake as directed above.

Added Goodies: Pie fillings are a great place to get creative. Try adding rum- or brandy-soaked raisins, chocolate chips, mini marshmallows, or toasted nuts to this sweet potato filling.

Port-Glazed Persimmons

MAKES ABOUT 4 SERVINGS

Although I love the persimmon in its natural state—sweet, juicy, with slight honey and date overtones—I love cooking with it even more. It is a surprisingly versatile fruit, as this recipe demonstrates.

Ingredients

3 Fuyu persimmons

1 cup dried Mission figs, quartered

1 pint fresh blueberries

2 cups port

½ cup granulated sugar

½ teaspoon kosher salt

1 teaspoon freshly ground roughly cracked black peppercorns (you can use the bottom of your skillet to break 'em up!)

1 cup crème fraîche

½ cup sliced almonds, toasted

Method

1. Preheat oven to 350°F. Spiralize persimmons using the straight blade to create flat spiral ribbons. Arrange in a baking dish with the figs and blueberries.

2. Add port to the baking dish, then sprinkle evenly with sugar, salt, and peppercorns. Bake until the juices are bubbly and the fruits begin to brown. Serve a warm spoonful of the baked fruits and their juice with a dollop of crème fraîche and sprinkle of toasted almonds.

Zucchini Bread

MAKES 2 MEDIUM SIZED LOAVES

If you ever grew zucchini in your garden, you are well-acquainted with this recipe. It is the go-to recipe for using up an abundant crop. Luckily for those of you without a green thumb, they sell zucchini at the market.

Ingredients

3–4 large zucchini (about 4 cups)

1⅔ cups brown sugar

⅔ cup vegetable oil

4 eggs

3 cups whole wheat flour (gluten-free flour works here, too)

½ teaspoon baking powder

2 teaspoons baking soda

1 teaspoon kosher salt

1 teaspoon cinnamon

2 teaspoons ground nutmeg

1 teaspoon cardamom

⅛ teaspoon ground clove

Method

1. Preheat oven to 350°F. Coat two 9 x 5-inch loaf pans with pan spray, and line them lengthwise with a strip of parchment paper or foil. Spiralize the zucchini into thin shreds, using the smallest holes. Set aside.

2. In a large bowl whisk together sugar, oil, and eggs. Mix in zucchini. Sift and add the flour, baking powder, baking soda, salt, and spices. Stir until just combined.

3. Transfer the batter to prepared pans. Bake for 30–40 minutes, until a pick inserted comes out clean. (Cover with foil if the crust gets too dark before the center is cooked.) Cool 10 minutes, then remove to a rack to prevent sweating. Serve warm or toasted with marmalade, sweet butter, or cream cheese.

VARIATIONS

Nuts and Fruit: Add up to 2 cups of raisins and/or nuts. Be sure to toast and cool your nuts for better flavor, and plump your raisins in hot water for 15–20 minutes.

Confetti Bread: Use 4 cups of mixed colored vegetables for a festive slice! Try carrot, beet, parsnip, and yellow squash in addition to the zucchini.

Glossary

Acidulated
The addition of acid. In cooking this most frequently references acidulated water, in which a small amount of lemon juice or vinegar is added to water (¼ cup per gallon of water is sufficient) to keep foods from oxidizing (turning brown).

Al dente
An Italian term that means "to the tooth," and refers to the degree to which certain foods—usually vegetables or pasta—are cooked. When cooked, these foods retain a slight texture when bitten. They are not crunchy, nor are they soft.

Amaretto
An Italian liqueur with the distinctive flavor of bitter almonds.

Andouille
French spiced and smoked sausage originally from the regions of Brittany and Normandy. When the French migrated to Nova Scotia, and then to Louisiana, their culinary traditions followed. The Cajun version of andouille is quite a bit hotter than its French counterpart.

Anise
An annual flowering herb, related to parsley. The seeds have a distinctive licorice flavor, which is used in liqueurs, candies, sauces, and cosmetics. Sweet anise is a name often used when referring to the bulb of the vegetable fennel. The two plants, however, are unrelated.

Béchamel
French white cream sauce made by adding milk to roux. It is one of the classic Mother Sauces.

Blanch
To boil briefly, then submerge in ice water to halt cooking. The process is used to loosen the skin, soften the flesh, and intensify the color of vegetables and fruits. Also referred to as parboiling.

Cajun seasoning
A blend of herbs and spices, widely available ready mixed, that typically includes garlic, onions, chiles, pepper, and mustard.

Candied ginger
Ginger root, cooked in sugar syrup, and coated in sugar.

Caramelized
To cook food until the sugar, naturally occurring or added, darkens to an amber "caramel" color. Caramelization brings out a food's deep, sweet, rich flavors.

Chiffonade
A leaf cut into thin, ribbonlike strips. It is achieved by stacking several leaves, rolling them like a cigar, and slicing off "coins" from one end of the cigar to the other. The technique is used frequently for basil and mint.

Coconut milk
The by-product of grating fresh coconut meat. The canned product is made by grating fresh coconut, then soaking it in hot water to extract the coconuts fat and flavor. There is no actual cow milk. Coconut milk is always unsweetened, unless specified otherwise. Cream of coconut is another product that is presweetened, and typically used for cocktails. The two are not interchangeable. Coconut water is still another product. Water naturally accumulates in the center of the nut as it grows. This water takes on a delicious coconut flavor, and is drunk right out of the fresh nut.

Creaming

Blending of two ingredients into a creamy, smooth, pastelike texture. Usually used in reference to the combination of butter and granulated sugar.

Cured/curing

A method of preserving food with salt (corned), acid (pickled), or smoke.

Currants

Tiny raisins made from the miniature zante grape. Do not confuse them with red, white, or black currants, which are small berries used for preserves, pastries, and the liqueur cassis.

Deglaze

A method of removing cooked food and its flavor from the bottom of a sauté or roasting pan by adding liquid, heating it, and scraping it.

Equator

In cooking this term refers to the center division of sphere-shaped produce. If we label the stem ends as north and south poles, the equator would be the horizontal cut across the middle. It is specified so that produce is cut in the right direction for the application. For instance, an orange is best juiced when cut across the equator because it opens up the individual sections, allowing more liquid to flow out.

Filberts

Another name for hazelnuts.

Folding

The gentle incorporation of two ingredients, one of which usually is a foam.

Fuji

A crisp, sweet Japanese apple variety introduced in the 1960s, popularized in the United States in the 1980s.

Ganache

A pastry kitchen staple ingredient, made from equal parts cream and chocolate, used for fillings, truffles, glazes, and icings.

Grand Marnier

A French liqueur made from a blend of cognac and oranges.

Herbes de Provence

An herb blend from the Provence region of France, frequently used in Mediterranean cuisine. It usually contains lavender, thyme, sage, marjoram, basil, rosemary, fennel, and savory.

Ice bath

Ice water used to quickly cool foods. Foods can be placed directly in the bath, or set on top in another bowl, and stirred until cool.

Julienne

A classic cut, often referred to as a matchstick, with a standard measurement of $\frac{1}{8}$ x $\frac{1}{8}$ x 2½ inches.

Kalamata

Greek black olives marinated in wine and olive oil.

Macerate

To soak food, usually fruit, in liquid, to infuse flavor.

Makrut lime leaves

This lime variety is used extensively throughout Asia both medicinally and in the preparation of food and spirits. But it is the hourglass, double-lobed leaf that is most prized. Used extensively throughout Thailand, Cambodia, Vietnam, Indonesia, Malaysia, Burma, and Laos, the leaf is highly pungent, and easily preserved. The variety has been known for decades in the West as the Kaffir Lime, until it was made clear that the K-word is considered derogatory hate speech in much of the world. Some stores now refer to these leaves simply as "lime leaves," but be careful. For cooking, the double-lobed leaf is the one with all the flavor.

Microplane

A fine grater used for citrus zest and hard cheeses. The tool was originally a carpenter's rasp used for sanding wood.

Parchment paper
Heavy paper that withstands heat, water, and grease, used to line pans and wrap foods.

Parboiling
See blanch.

Reduce
To cook the water out of a dish, reducing its volume, intensifying its flavor, and thickening its consistency.

Roux
A thickening agent made with equal parts of fat (usually butter) and flour.

Sauté
To cook food quickly, over high heat, constantly stirring for even browning. The term is French, and it means "to jump." Sauté pans are designed with a curved lip, making constant motion as easy as a flick of the wrist.

Shallot
A member of the onion family. It grows in large cloves, similar to garlic, has multiple layers, like onions, and a reddish brown papery skin. The flavor is more subtle than both.

Simple syrup
A pastry staple ingredient, made by boiling equal parts sugar and water. Used for moistening cakes, sweetening sauces and fruit purees, and as a recipe ingredient.

Sriracha
A Vietnamese sauce made from hot chiles, garlic, vinegar, and salt. It is often referred to as "rooster sauce," a reference to the rooster on the label of the best-selling brand, Huy Fong.

Stone fruit
A tree fruit that contains a pit, or stone, such as peaches, apricots, cherries, and plums.

Supremes
1. A section of citrus fruit that has been removed from its membrane. To get at the supreme, cut the top and bottom off the fruit, cut off all the skin so that no white pith is visible (so the fruit looks naked) then slice out each section with a sharp knife.
2. The small piece of chicken muscle attached to the breast, sometimes called the tender.

Water bath
A method in which a pan of food is cooked resting in another, larger pan of water (as in a baked custard). The method slows the conduction of heat, cooking slowly and gently. Also known in French as a bain marie.

Zest
The colorful outermost rind of a citrus fruit, containing high concentration of the essential oils and flavor compounds that flavor the fruit itself. The best way to access this is with a microplane.

Acknowledgments

Thanks to BJ Berti at St. Martin's Press and Katherine Latshaw at Folio for their unwavering support. All the food writers I know are jealous of my editor and agent. And to Teri Lyn Fisher, whose talent is surpassed only by her professionalism and friendship. Finally to Bill, Emma, and Claire, who are always my biggest supporters.

Index